FROM WHALEBONE TO HOT HOUSE

A Journey Along North Carolina's
Longest Highway, U.S. 64

FROM WHALEBONE TO HOT HOUSE

A Journey Along North Carolina's Longest Highway, U.S. 64

Jerry Bledsoe

The East Woods Press

Charlotte, North Carolina

Library of Congress Cataloging-in-Publication Data

Bledsoe, Jerry.
    From whalebone to hothouse.

    1. North Carolina—Description and travel—1981-
2. Unites States Highway 64. 3. Bledsoe, Jerry—
Journeys—North Carolina. I. Title.
F260.B576   1986   917.56'0443   86-45576
ISBN 0-88742-106-7

Cover design by Kenn Compton
Typography by Raven Type
Printed in the United States of America

East Woods Press Books
Fast & McMillan Publishers, Inc.
429 East Boulevard
Charlotte, NC 28203

Foreword

This book is about a five-month trip I took along U.S. 64, North Carolina's longest highway, a trip I hoped would allow me to capture the essence of my home state in words.

Near the end of my trip, Dot Mason of the Cherokee County Welcome Center told me something that shouldn't have come as a surprise. When many foreign travel agents have customers who want to see the "real" America, she said, they route them into the Atlanta airport, put them on buses, drive them north to Murphy, then across North Carolina, the state that they believe to be a microcosm of America.

In the depths of the mountains, it's hard to imagine that the surf, sand dunes and murky swamps of the east are in the same state. To get an idea of just how broad North Carolina is, consider this. If you live in Murphy and want to go to the beach, it's closer to go to Florida's panhandle beaches than to North Carolina's. New York is closer to Raleigh than Manteo is to Murphy.

My trip confirmed for me what I already knew: North Carolina truly is a remarkable and beautiful place. That, no doubt, is why it has become a people magnet, not only for vacationers but for people wanting to start new lives. People are moving to the state from every section of the country and other lands as well, but particularly from northern states and Florida. They are coming in large numbers and bringing dramatic change with them.

When I met these newcomers, they invariably spoke of the warmth of their reception. The warmth of North Carolina's people is something to which I surely can attest. Only once in my trip did I get turned away by somebody I stopped to visit. That was in Princeville at a house with piles of old bricks in the front yard and a sign offering for sale, at $3 each, original bricks from the demolished home of the man for whom the town was named, Turner Prince. That guy was holding out for a TV contract before he'd talk about those bricks.

It never ceases to amaze me that people not only will welcome a stranger but tell him intimate details about their lives. I thank all of those in this book for doing just that, as well as scores of others with whom I talked on my trip but who didn't make the book.

While I'm expressing appreciation, I am especially grateful to the editors of the Greensboro News & Record who made it possible for me to take this trip and allowed me to reprint the material in this book.

Jerry Bledsoe, April, 1986

In memory of Roy Rabon, Jr.,
who lived on U.S. 64 and loved it

Contents

Introduction

It begins without fanfare, a swooping curve at a place called Whalebone and suddenly the signs are different. No longer is the highway U.S. 158. It has become U.S. 64-264.

Here in sand and scrub growth, within sound of the Atlantic surf, begins North Carolina's longest highway, U.S. 64. For some 600 miles it divides the state lengthwise, slicing it diagonally from the sand dunes of the Northeast to the mountains of its southwesternmost tip, emerging into the copper mining country of Tennessee near a community called Isabella. From there it continues on through Tennessee, Arkansas and Oklahoma more than 2,200 miles until it ends at the intersection of U.S. 550 at Farmington in northwest New Mexico.

Through all of North Carolina's widely varied terrain and 24 of its 100 counties, the highway passes, catching only edges of Pitt, Franklin and McDowell, a narrow section of Jackson. It connects 20 county seats with the state's capital.

"If you can walk with me through the paths of time," Bill Burbage, a State Transportation Department record keeper, says with a smile as he places a big book of old highway maps on his desk. "Here's 1920. That map doesn't have any numbers on it."

We are trying to find when the highway came into existence. Records and history are short on the subject. Through the years, Bill flips. "1929," he says. "Not there."

But other U.S. highways make their appearances in the state that year—1, 15, 17, 21, 25, 70, 74, 221, 321, 421.

"Now watch this," Bill says, holding back a map. "1932 was no different. When we hit this 1933 map, we're picking up 64 for the first time. This map, we're seeing the old numbers, too. It's got both of them on there."

Who picked the route for 64 is unknown at the Transportation Department and not found in history books. The history of many individual roads is lost, and 64, like other U.S. highways, is just a hodgepodge of once local roads.

In 1914, North Carolina had 4,313 miles of roads, none paved, most of them little more than rutted lanes, all but impassable in wet weather, all maintained by individual counties. In 1915, the General

11

Assembly created the State Highway Commission to help counties build a system of roads that would connect all principal towns and county seats. In 1921, a $50 million bond sale was approved to construct 5,500 miles of roads and $65 million more was approved over the next six years.

Although it didn't reach North Carolina for a few years, the U.S. highway numbering system was devised in 1926 to make interstate travel easier.

"People think there's a difference in funding for U.S. routes and N.C. routes," says Charlie Atkins of the State Transportation Department, "but there's not. It's just a numbering scheme for convenience."

In 1931, when the state assumed responsibility for roads from the counties—by then more than 45,000 miles, only 913 miles paved—what would become U.S. 64 two years later was a series of roads across the state.

From Columbia on the Scuppernong River in desolate coastal Tyrell County westward to Statesville in foothills Iredell County, it was state road 90. From Statesville to Marion in mountainous McDowell County, it was state road 10 and U.S. 70. From Marion southward to Rutherfordton, where it picked up U.S. 74, it was state road 19. At Bat Cave in Henderson County, it became state road 28 to the Tennessee line.

Not until 1950 did the highway extend eastward into water-isolated Dare County on the coast to the point where it now begins south of Nags Head.

In its passage across the state, U.S. 64 is as varied as the terrain. At some points it follows the path of Indian trails. Along the Albemarle Sound it once was a colonial road, one of the state's and nation's oldest highways. Its route has changed many times as improvements were made and new bypasses built.

At some spots, it is a two-lane country road with hardly a shoulder. At others it is broad and modern, built to interstate standards. In its newest stretch, looping with several other highways around the south side of Raleigh, it is eight lanes wide and isolated from its surroundings by high, intimidating concrete walls.

In east and west, it remains a more vital artery than in the Piedmont, where Interstate 40 has assumed much of its former burden. Nevertheless, its sheer length and the areas through which it passes make it the highway most representative of the state.

Wash Baum's Dream: The First Mile

WHALEBONE   Wash Baum didn't want people to know what he was up to. He knew what their reaction likely would be. At first, he led everybody to believe it was just a canal the county was building.

Wash knew that the automobile was bringing drastic change to the country that eventually would reach even into isolated Dare County. With its beautiful beaches on the Outer Banks, the county had great potential, he knew, if only people could get there. But roads and bridges would have to be built, particularly bridges. As chairman of the county commissioners, Wash already had appealed to the state for help and had been turned down. It would be up to the county, he decided, to connect itself with the rest of the world, and he set about seeing that it did.

He started with a causeway and bridge across Roanoke Sound, linking Roanoke Island and the county seat, Manteo, to the beaches, where transportation was still largely by foot, boat, horse and cart.

When people finally discovered what Wash was really doing, a cry of protest arose. Some accused Wash of trying to ruin the county financially, but he continued with his road and bridge and opened it with a toll of a dollar a car in 1928.

Some people derided it, calling it the bridge to nowhere, and indeed where it ended on Bodie Island, only a series of trails led off in different directions into the dunes.

At exactly that spot, Alexander Midgett built his service station. He sold Esso gas from hand pumps and did a big business in fishing tackle.

"He was the first service station on the beach," says his son, Oscar, a retired Coast Guardsman who operates Dixie's Kitchen in Manteo, the first down-home cafe on U.S. 64. ("The seats are for your seat; the floor is for your feet," advises a hand-lettered sign over a booth. "Keep them so.")

Oscar is a burly man with tattoos of exotic ladies on both arms. After he retired from service, he worked for a fish company and on tugboats until a heart attack convinced him that he should find easier work. So he bought the cafe from Betty Edwards, renamed it for his wife, and now comes in every morning at 4:30, seven days a week, and leaves at 2 p.m. when his wife takes over. "Lots of hours here," he says, "but it's not the work, it's just the hours."

He was three when his father died, so he has no memories of him, but he does remember the whale.

"Seventy-two foot," he says, taking a break from frying eggs. At a front table, a group of locals are playing country songs on the juke box and having beer for breakfast. "My daddy way back there years ago brought that whale off the beach with a old Model T Ford. Had him up on a scaffold."

Alexander Midgett dragged that monstrous blue whale off the beach in 1930, a year before the state finally built the first road along the beach, connecting Wash Baum's bridge to another toll bridge that had been built across Currituck Sound 17 miles northward. He mounted its bones by the roadside. They became a big tourist attraction and gave a name not only to his service station but to the place that eventually would mark the beginning of U.S. Highway 64.

Alexander Midgett's gas station is gone now. His wife, Neva, who came to be known to beachgoers as Mama Midgett, operated it after her husband's death in 1935 until it burned in 1941. The whale bones were carted away, most stolen piece by piece. Mama Midgett had a 15-foot jawbone and several sections of backbone moved to the yard of a tourist home she operated in Manteo until her death in 1965. A few years later, a grandson gave the bones to the Marine Resources Center near Manteo, where they are now displayed.

The first business on U.S. 64 now is RV's, a fancy restaurant and lounge, two years old, designed to appeal to tourists—one of six seafood restaurants along the four-mile causeway to the beach that Wash Baum built. RV's is not yet open on this morning, but next door Blackbeard's Treasure Chest is.

Between customers, Elmo and Elsie Williams are busy trying to get ready for a new beach season.

"This place has been a restaurant, service station, antique shop, shell shop and I don't know what all," Elmo says. "Had rental rooms years ago, I guess. There were eight or 10 bathrooms in the place when we got it."

For 30 years, Elmo was a service station operator in Virginia. He had one of the busiest stations in Hampton, sold 235,000 gallons a month, employed 13 people and was prosperous enough to buy a cottage on the beach at Kitty Hawk 14 years ago.

"Oil companies gobbled me up," he says. "Lost my lease after years of business."

"When people started pumping their own gas," says Elsie, "I told my husband then, I said 'Something's going to happen,' and it did."

In his 50s, without a job for the first time in his life, Elmo retreated with Elsie to the beach to contemplate the future. That's when they saw the shell shop for sale. They bought it and immediately began knocking out walls, expanding, adding jewelry, T-shirts, souvenirs, gifts, crafts. Elsie, a decorator, began making decorator items. The shop became a year-round business for both of them. But now, as they begin their ninth year in it, the shop is for sale.

14

"We're going to retire," Elsie says. "We're old enough to retire. We've worked all our lives."

"We'll do a little something on the side," Elmo says with a grin. "Keep from getting rusty."

The Melvin R. Daniels Bridge is the first on the highway, just a couple of hundred feet long, spanning a channel through the causeway. Unlike the nearly mile-long Washington Baum Bridge, which crosses the main part of the sound just up the road, fishing is allowed from the Daniels Bridge.

This day, its only occupants are a clan from Manassas, Va.: Mel Snyder, his wife and three daughters and their husbands and children. Mel works at Dulles International Airport receiving jet fuel. For 15 years, he has brought his family to vacation on the Outer Banks every spring, usually staying at a nearby pier. This time the family is staying in a cottage at Duck, 20 miles away, but they've come to this bridge to fish and crab because they've always done it.

"We was out there on the pier this morning but we didn't catch anything. Too windy," Mel says, as he slices the sides of a small perch, then pierces one eye and the side with a wire and fastens it to the bottom of a small crab trap. "Cut 'em up so the crabs can get ahold of 'em. Lady on the pier gave us the fish."

He'd already set two traps, tied to the bridge with rope, and now he's preparing two more. His son-in-law, Martin Downs, reels in a croaker and Mel's 12-year-old grandson, Jimmy, brings it to him for more bait.

"We've caught some nice crabs out here," Mel says. "When they're running, you can catch two or three dozen nice big blue crabs."

His wife, Margaret, pulls up one trap and two startled crabs dance about inside. Jimmy retrieves them from the trap, grabbing them from behind and showing them to a frightened younger cousin while Mel fetches his measuring stick.

"He's too little," Mel says of the first and Jimmy tosses him back. "He's almost but not quite," Mel says of the second, which is also spared.

"We take and steam 'em when they're big enough," Mel says. "Put vinegar and Old Bay seasoning and steam 'em until they turn red and then you got some fine eatin'. We get a big bucketful and tonight we'll invite you for dinner. Then tomorrow, you'll be out here."

"Just a minute," Sally Wadsworth says, peeking into the motel office from the door of her adjoining apartment. "I'm feeding dogs."

She emerges shortly, smiling. "My son has one and I have one," she says of the dogs. "We have two too many. One is a schnauzer. The other is a nuisance."

For years, Sally and her husband, a Bertie County farmer, had a cottage at the beach. Six years ago, Sally began looking for an investment and bought the Fin 'N Feather, a two-story motel with a blue brick facade. It has five rooms with double beds, five efficiencies with double beds and the apartment where Sally lives alone except when her husband comes on weekends.

This is the only motel on the causeway, the first on U.S. 64. Sally, who spent 15 years working in a bank, operates it year-round with the help of a single maid.

"Love it," she says. "Love it. Anytime you're your own boss, you know . . . . It doesn't take all my time. Had you come this morning, you wouldn't have found anyone. I fish. I ride jet skis. I go boating."

She suffers no lack of business. Beachgoers fill the rooms in summer, fishermen in spring and fall, duck hunters in winter. More visitors come every year and more people move into the area. Development marches apace. And although such growth is good for Sally financially, she watches it with some trepidation and wonders where it all is leading.

On the day before had come news of a motel on the beach dumping raw sewage into a ditch. Nearby waters are often closed to shellfishing because of contamination.

Sally talks about the problems as she looks out the window at the causeway Wash Baum built and the nearby bridge that bears his name, along which runs the road that opened the fragile area to development.

"I fear," she says, "that we're making a cesspool for our descendants."

Life From The Sand

WHALEBONE   The old house sits fast by the sound, two stories tall, covered with white gypsum siding, the first house on Highway 64. The front porch has been transformed into a greenhouse of plastic panels and storm windows where tomato plants and petunias grow. The yard is a clutter of machine parts.

"It's one of the oldest buildings in the county, I think," John Korbach says as he sits in the living room, thumbing through books looking for information on the house. He's never known when it was built, only that it was a hunting lodge called the Lone Cedar Club.

"As far as I know it was a bunch of lawyers and doctors out of Philadelphia," he says. "Had their own guns made up to suit 'em. Anyway, it was way back. I don't know who the heck I can find out from."

Whatever its origins, the house became John's home 22 years ago.

"Because of a shipwreck," he says with a laugh.

It's a story he delights in telling.

John followed his father into the construction business in Norfolk. They built apartments, restaurants, what have you. When John contracted to build a yacht club, he decided to save money by dredging the basin himself. That required a dredge.

"Built that dredge from scratch," he says. It is tied up now in the sound behind the house, its upper structure visible through the sliding glass door that John installed last fall. "That's an old 50-foot landing barge that I got in '45 and rigged it up as a dredge. She's a historical landmark as far as I'm concerned. Haven't used her in three or four years."

The dredge led John into marine salvage work. He loved the challenge of floating vessels, freeing grounded barges. In 1961, he heard about a 68-foot fishing trawler, the Sarah J, that had run aground, split open and been abandoned on her side, half sunk in the treacherous waters of Oregon Inlet. John decided to salvage her. She was part of a dream.

Sand was in big demand in the Bahamas then. John wanted to take his dredge there and start a sand company. He wanted the Sarah J as a supply boat to run back and forth to the mainland.

Raising the boat was tricky work, most of it underwater in dangerous currents. Seven weeks it took just to suck out the 50,000 pounds of decayed flounder in the hold.

"Stuck together like huge mats," John recalls, going into details about how he did it and the pain it caused him.

17

John Korbach on his dredge

At the end of the eighth week, he floated her.

"Had her up, had her ready to go and a hurricane hit. I mean she was blowing a gale. Had to turn it loose."

The storm sank the Sarah J again. This time she was beyond salvage, and so was John's Bahamas dream.

He was driving into Manteo after the storm thinking about what he would do next when he saw the "for sale" sign in front of the old house on the causeway connecting the beaches with Roanoke Island.

The weeks he'd spent at Oregon Inlet had rekindled fond memories of all the fishing trips he'd made to the Outer Banks with his father as a boy.

"I realized I'd learned to love this area," he says. "I said to myself, 'If I can't go to the Bahamas, I'll just settle here.' I stopped and kicked the "for sale" sign over, went home that night and called the owner, met him in Raleigh the next day and bought it. That's the best thing I ever did in my whole life."

With the house, which John got at a price that now seems hard to believe, came nearly a mile of land on the north side of the causeway and a small piece on the south side. Into the house he moved his wife, Jo, and five children, the eldest a daughter, Karen, then 15, the youngest a son, Kevin, then entering first grade.

At first John took jobs dredging, building piers and bulkheads. Then he built a service station across from his house and later added a Western Auto Store in it, which his wife and children helped operate.

"Selling blood worms and beer in a Western Auto," he says with a grin.

He sold that business six years ago. Then he sold a lot at the eastern end of his property for another service station. Last fall, he sold his last piece of land on the south side of the causeway for a restaurant. He could live out his days comfortably on his take from the last sale alone. No longer does he have to work.

"But I'm working harder than ever," he says, his eyes showing delight through thick glasses. "I play with flowers and garden, raise chickens. Got me 100 chickens. We ate the first one last night, and that's good chicken, boy. I've got a dumb nectarine tree out here, I don't believe that dumb thing. That's the craziest tree I've ever seen in my whole life. Come on, you've got to see that tree."

John knows some think that he is, if not as crazy as his nectarine tree, at least a little eccentric. Maybe it's because of the intensity he puts into growing things and creating things from odd bits of machinery. Maybe it's because of the way he looks—a short, balding man who's almost always dressed in old tennis shoes, baggy pants splotched with grease and paint and a construction worker's hard hat. But more likely it's because they find it hard to conceive somebody who's perfectly content raising apples, peaches, pears, nectarines, grapes, asparagus and chickens on some of the most valuable business land in North Carolina.

"Eighty-six different grapevines," he says, pointing out his vine-yards on the way to the crazy nectarine tree. "Don't tell me you can't grow things in sand. All you need is sun, sand and a little ingenuity. Look at the size of that asparagus. Isn't that pretty?"

He snatches a white radish from a lush row, wipes off the sand and crunches into it.

"I put fish in here," he says. "And chicken manure. I go to Columbia and get a trailer load at a time. I've put as much as a thousand fish in here at one time. I've got three blue marlin in here that would weigh over a thousand pounds. Here's that dumb tree. It is four years old and I don't believe it. I just don't believe the dumb tree. I've never seen anything grow like that in my life."

It is amazingly big and lush and loaded with fruit.

"Look at all those dumb nectarines."

Later, while John is showing off the ingenious chicken house he built, petting a favorite chicken named Little Bit that follows him wherever he goes, he glances at the sky and sees a bird floating over the edge of the sound.

"Watch that bird right there. That's the best fisherman in the world," he says, then calls to his son, working nearby. "There's the old osprey up there, Jack, waiting to get his fish. He'll get it, too.

"You see why I love this place so much? No body has any idea how much the Korbach family has enjoyed this place. It opened the door to a beautiful, beautiful life for this family, I tell you."

The Fisherman

MANTEO   At midmorning, the green and white wooden boat, 16 feet long and 20 years old, came putt-putting back up the narrow canal cut into the marsh.

Wilbur Rogers steered it to the edge and tied it at the little squatter's dock beside a stretch of abandoned road alongside Highway 64.

A short day. He'd gone out at 7, was back several hours early.

"Too rough out there," he said.

He removed the top of his slicker to reveal a red plaid wool shirt. It had been a cold morning for May, the wind blowing hard from the north. White caps danced over the sound, sending up sheets of spray as Wilbur's boat, powered by a 10 horsepower motor, wallowed through the swells. The slicker had kept the spray off but it was a case of getting wet from without or wet from within.

"I'm soaking wet," he said. "I get wet with sweat."

He made it to all of his nets this morning, set nets anchored in the shallow sound. Fish swim into them and get caught by the gills. He has six nets ranging from 20 yards long to 80. He has 40 crab pots, too, but most of them would have to wait until another day to be emptied and rebaited.

"Little bit too rough this morning to fish the pots. I got to about half of 'em."

His voice, with its unique Outer Banks accent, betrays his roots. He was born in Duck, a remote village on the northern Banks. From age 10 until he went into the Army, he lived in Collington, a fishing village on a small island back of Kill Devil Hills. His father was a fisherman who taught his son the trade.

"Been fishing off and on all my life," he said. "When I was 10 years old, I used to walk up and down these edges and catch soft crabs and double crabs. Used to be a feller down at the end of the bridge bought 'em for 5 cents a piece. Now they get about 40 cents."

Wilbur went off to World War II, got shot up in the battle of New Guinea and came home to fish, with pains he knew he'd have to bear. In 1952, he left the Banks and moved to Virginia, where for 10 years he was a policeman, although he knew all along that wasn't right for him.

"I wanted to come back and go fish," he says, and he did.

Carpentry and bricklaying occupied him when he wasn't able to fish, and once more he moved inland, this time to Gates County where for three years he helped his son in the aluminum siding business. But divorcing himself from the water, he found, was

21

Wilbur Rogers bringing in the catch

something he couldn't do.

Five years ago, he'd returned to fish again. He moved to Manteo, bought the old boat, got some nets and crab pots and built himself a little dock on the canal where other fishermen and crabbers tie up small boats.

"Everywhere I went, I always came back," he said. "The work suits me. Nobody bothers me. I just enjoy it."

The question is how much longer he'll be able to enjoy it. It is hard, everyday work. "You gotta go seven a days a week or you lose everything. Seagulls and crabs eat up the fish and a lot of people that ain't got nothing to do but steal goes out and steals your crabs." And time is catching up with him.

He is 61 now, and there are days when he just can't go. "Had arthritis so bad I had to quit last year," he said. "Ain't able to do much."

Besides, if things continue the way they've been going, there could be little point in continuing.

"Over in this area, it's getting worse all the time," he says of the fishing. "Ever since that Oregon Inlet filled up, ain't much fish comes in here. If you had enough equipment and everything, you could do all right, I guess. The people that's got nice boats and all, I don't think they have any trouble making a living. I make enough to get by and that's it."

The catch this day was not good, but not bad either, considering the weather.

"About medium," he said. "Mostly blue fish. One big speckled trout. Couple mullet. Two croakers."

He also had a few dozen jimmies, big male crabs, and from the shedding cages floating next to the dock, he picked out a couple of dozen soft crabs.

"See, this is the peeler season right now," he said. "People catchin' peelers to shed out and make soft crabs."

He set about sorting the catch into white plastic buckets. Little blues in one, big in another. The big trout with the croakers and mullet. Into another bucket went fish mangled by crabs and gulls to become bait for crab traps tomorrow.

"Gotta get these to the market," he said. "That's why I'm in such a rush."

He sells to a retail market on the beach because it pays cash on the spot. The big fish companies keep a record and send a check later.

With the fish sorted, the boat secured, Wilbur took off his oil pants, removed the motor from the back of the boat and shoved it onto the dock. He loaded everything into a rusty Plymouth station wagon.

"Yeah," he said, before pulling away. "I guess you could say I just like to fish. Never did make much money. Had a lot of fun, though. I'm satisfied. Might as well be. This is all I'm going to get."

Sailing Into History

MANTEO   He must have been an awfully adventurous or inno-
cent man, the Indian who walked alone along the beach and
approached the alien vessels that July day 400 years ago.

Surely the two large ships were fearsome with their strange crews,
fair-skinned and hairy, grandly dressed and bearing exotic arms.

But the Indian approached with gestures of friendliness and one
of the ships sent out a small boat, brought him aboard, gave him
food and drink and a tour of the ship. When he returned to the
beach, he went into the inlet in his dugout canoe, filled it with fish
and left them on the beach in two piles, a gift for each ship.

Next day, a large group of Indian men appeared on the beach
with a leader named Granganimeo and welcomed the visitors. That
is how English explorers were first received in this country, in a
place that eventually would be known as North Carolina. (At first
the English called it Wingandacon, because that's what an Indian
responded when a crew member asked what this place was called.
Wingandacon, the English later learned, meant "you wear good
clothes.")

The men on those two ships, sent by Sir Walter Raleigh to find a
suitable place for a colony, later were received hospitably at an
Indian village on Roanoke Island. They returned to England with
favorable reports and two Indians who befriended them, Manteo
and Wanchese. The following year more than 300 Englishmen,
mostly soldiers, showed up on Roanoke Island and more than 100
stayed, built an earthen fort and log houses and established the first
English colony in America.

More interested in treasure and profit than making a life, these
men found hardship, created trouble with the Indians and eagerly
abandoned their settlement the following year, when English war-
ships on the way home from fighting the Spanish in Florida offered
them passage. The ship bringing supplies to the men found the
colony abandoned and 15 men were left to hold it for another year.

Meanwhile, Raleigh organized another group of more than 100
men, women and children to settle the colony. The group arrived
in July 1587 and found the 15 men had disappeared mysteriously,
just as they would be found to have done three years later. This
group became known as the Lost Colony and ended British attempts
to settle the area that now is North Carolina. Not until nearly two
decades later did the English establish a successful colony at James-
town in Virginia.

Horace Whitfield, Captain of Elizabeth II

Once again a ship like those that brought the first English colonists rides the waters by Roanoke Island. This is the *Elizabeth II*, a 69-foot three-masted bark, centerpiece of North Carolina's commemoration of those voyages 400 years ago.

At this moment, the ship is tilted to her starboard side, her ballast shifted so that volunteers may paint along the water line on her port side. A small group of tourists watches the work near a small dock, and as the ship's captain rows ashore in a dinghy, they accost him.

After the captain has answered all their questions, one woman looks at him admiringly and says, "I just envy you so much."

"I'll let you bring that ship to the dock one time and see how envious you are," he says with a smile. "I haven't been tried yet. I'm just like that ship. I'm sitting here ready to go."

The captain is Horace Whitfield, a friendly, bearded man of 33, former English teacher at Manteo High School. Son of a newspaper editor, Horace grew up in Raleigh reading about the sea and sailing ships. At East Carolina University he studied journalism and English. After his junior year, he went sailing for the first time—on a reservoir near Indianapolis where he was working on a summer project.

After graduation, he moved to Manteo, worked odd jobs at marinas before he began to teach, rebuilt an old crabbing skiff and converted it to sail, then built himself a 26-foot sail boat, *Greedless*, and sailed away to Florida for seven months.

Back in Manteo, he married and worked as a boat builder. He was fascinated when he heard that a replica of an old English ship was to be built in Manteo and applied for the job of captain. He was hired two years ago so he could observe the ship's construction, and he couldn't be happier about his job.

"I love the ship and I love sailing and I love working with people and this job allows me to do all of that," he says.

For now the job consists of maintaining the ship, training the crew, answering tourists' questions and preparing for the opening of the ship and the new visitor center on what used to be called Ice Plant Island across from the Manteo waterfront. The ship can't sail yet because Shallowbag Bay is too shallow, but a new channel is to be dredged to the bay and Horace is hopeful that the ship will be able to sail for the first time to other North Carolina ports.

"To me, the sailing is going to be the highlight," he says. "There's no manual to sailing this kind of ship. A lot of the seamanship has been lost to time. We're relearning things. I'm not afraid of her, but there's a lot I'm sure that we don't know about. We'll kind of have to play it by ear."

The First Town

MANTEO   Construction begins as the highway turns northward on Roanoke Island and enters Manteo. The road is being widened, curbed, repaved, its edges seeded with grass.

Manteo is gussying up to celebrate the arrival of English settlers on the island 400 years ago.

Actually, the town has been getting ready for a long time. Once it was just a country town, hardly distinguishable from other country towns except that it was on an island. But a few years back the town got to imagining itself an English village. Building owners put up Old English facades and quaint "shoppes" opened calling themselves "Ye Olde" this and that. Even Doris Walker, who started Walker's Grill in a 13-seat surplus Navy bus that grew into a full-fledged restaurant, dressed up her place and started calling it Duchess of Dare.

Now, condominiums are going up on the town's waterfront, the penalty, perhaps, for pretension.

In the midst of all the construction debris stands the figure of Sir Walter Raleigh, who sent the first English settlers to the island. At least it's supposed to be Sir Walter, although it hardly resembles portraits of him.

The figure was chiseled from the trunk of a 507-year-old cypress tree 10 years ago in a Raleigh shopping center by a flamboyant character who called himself the Tree Carver. He decided to carve Sir Walter because he happened to be carving in Raleigh, but people who watched the figure's progress over the 10 months it took to complete it noted that it looked more like the Tree Carver duded up in 16th-century attire than Sir Walter.

Proclaimed the world's largest wooden sculpture, the statue stood 24 feet tall, weighed 15,000 pounds, and nobody seemed to know what to do with it until somebody suggested donating it to the town of Manteo, where it was erected in the little Bicentennial Park.

Now, Sir Walter is not in the best of shape. A woodpecker carved out a nest under his right rib cage sometime back, and his rear end is in a serious state of deterioration. So far, nobody has made any move to gussy him up for the big celebration.

On the northern edge of Manteo, a highway sign appears: "Murphy 543." It is more a gimmick than a source of information. For years the phrase "from Manteo to Murphy" has been used to describe the breadth of North Carolina. It was convenient that the easternmost and westernmost towns of size in the state were not only alliterative but also on the same highway.

The sign, by the way, isn't accurate—just a guess. The State Transportation Department isn't sure of the exact mileage. The information is in its computers, but it would be an involved process to get it—not worth the effort.

Two and a half miles north of town is the entrance to Fort Raleigh, site of the first English settlement. Here, in 1587, colonists built the "Cittie" of Raleigh, which disappeared with its builders who became known as the Lost Colony. The exact site of the settlement remains lost. Archaeologists never have been able to find it, but they'll make another attempt later this year.

The colonists' earthen fort has been reconstructed on its original site, though, and nearby is a visitors' center with a museum, an authentic 16th-century room shipped from England and a theater where a film about the colonists is shown regularly.

Nearby, at the Elizabethan Gardens, built by the Garden Club of North Carolina in 1951, visitors may see how the queen who authorized Sir Walter to send his expeditions to North Carolina dressed—ostentatiously. But it did little good for Elizabeth, a pale, frail woman with a little bird mouth, homely despite her baubles and finery.

Another work of art that may be viewed in the gardens is a sculptress's marble vision of how Virginia Dare, first English child born in America, might have looked if she had grown to young womanhood with a distaste for attire. Poor naked Virginia was shunted around to several places before finally finding a home in the gardens (Roanoke Island seems to be a haven for unwanted statues) where she now stands under a live oak tree staring with blank eyes, ignoring the big spiders that have made a home in her left ear.

Also in the midst of the formal gardens can be seen a patch of humble uppowoc, a plant the Indians introduced to the colonists, a plant later settlers of North Carolina used to build an economy. The English called it tobacco.

The Storekeepers

MANN'S HARBOR   It's a road to nowhere now, this short strip that used to be the main highway. Lined with decaying docks, tipsy fishing shanties and overgrown, tumbledown buildings, it goes to the old ferry landing, no longer used.

From the landing, traffic can be seen whizzing across Croatan Sound on the William B. Umstead Memorial Bridge, which connected Roanoke Island to the mainland years ago.

The ferry landing site may be old, but the landing itself is new, hurriedly rebuilt a year and a half ago when a runaway barge knocked out two sections of the bridge and brought the ferry back to life for two months, long months if you ask people who had been using the bridge daily.

It was at this landing that Stanford and Grace White saw opportunity nearly 50 years ago. They had run away to get married, and for a while they lived in Washington, D.C., but homesickness set in and they soon returned to Mann's Harbor and opened a little store at the landing to serve the travelers who often waited there for the ferry.

"At first we just had sardines and crackers and potted meat and cold drinks," Grace recalls, "and then we added on a little more and a little more. I started a snack bar. The ferry would stop and there was no place to eat and we'd make sandwiches."

Talk of the coming bridge eventually caused the Whites to sell the store, which washed into the sound in a storm years ago. Stanford went into the garage business with his father, then started a small ice plant. Grace took care of their three boys.

"But I liked the store business," Grace says, "and I decided I didn't want to loaf."

So she got her husband to build another small store, this one on the highway on the western approach to Mann's Harbor. Like the first store, this one started small and grew. As the Whites prospered, they expanded into other businesses. They built cottages to rent to fishermen (Stanford knew lots of fishermen because he was a game warden for years), and a small motel. They started a trailer park that grew to 100 spaces. And the little store became not so little and not just an ordinary store.

The Whites added hardware, appliances, fishing and hunting gear, clothing, shoes, toys, auto parts, gifts and souvenirs, and Grace started another grill in one corner.

They had so many different things that Stanford put a big sign across the front of the building: "Welcome. Inside 10,099 items to choose from."

"My husband used to have the reputation of stocking anything anybody wanted," Grace says. "We just had everything."

As business grew, Stanford became an influential man, a county commissioner, a state legislator. And White's Shopping Center became the commercial hub of mainland Dare County, one of the most desolate and sparsely populated areas in the state. At Christmas it even drew people from Manteo and the beach communities on the Outer Banks.

"We were the first ones in Dare County to have a Santy Claus," Grace says proudly. "The cars would be lined up from here to the corner. They'd be so crowded in here I'd have to push my way around to wait on people."

"We'd probably sell 50 bicycles during Christmas," says the White's son, Wade. "Now we don't even have 'em."

They have no Santa either.

"You've probably got a hundred Santa Clauses in 15 miles of here," Wade says in explanation.

Stanford is retired now, but his sign still boasts the store's variety, and the stock more than matches the claim. But business isn't what it once was. People in the area now can drive a few miles to bigger shopping centers in Manteo.

"Too much competition," says Wade. "Roses. K mart. It's called the big squeeze."

It makes Wade wonder how long the store can continue as it is.

"You can't afford nowadays to carry everything anybody wants," he says.

"I know times has changed in the last 30 years," his mother says, "but your daddy's always liked to have things when people want 'em."

Wade is 34, the youngest son. One of his brothers, Ray, became an executive with a big bank. The other, Stan, is a builder and real estate agent on the beach. Wade has been left to assume the family businesses, but his heart isn't in it.

"I hate it," he says of the work at the store. "This is a seven-day-a-week job, and it's from daylight to dark, and that's why I don't like it. Dadgum it, you can't get out of it."

"He don't like to be cooped up," says his mother. "But me, I enjoy it. I just like meeting people. There's some people been coming here for years, these fishermen. It's kind of sad, because so many of them have died. I feel like they're more friends than customers. To me, it's been real, real rewarding.

"I don't want to retire. Just as long as I'm able to stay on my feet, I want to work. I think it's good for a person to stay active. If I was to go to my home and stay and do housework, I think I'd be dead."

The Music of the Bridge

ALLIGATOR BRIDGE   "Good to see a human being," Kevin Roughton says with a smile. "It's nice to have company. I always appreciate anybody who stops in. I'm a people person. I don't really appreciate the isolation out here."

Isolation he has aplenty, perched in the small tower in the middle of the mouth of the Alligator River. The concrete tower sits on the edge of the Lindsay C. Warren Bridge, three miles long, the longest bridge on U.S. 64. From it, Kevin opens and closes the bridge's draw section, which straddles the Intracoastal Waterway.

He is having a busy day. It is yacht migration season. Playtoys for the rich dot the southern horizon, all heading to home ports in the North from Florida, the Bahamas and other points south.

"We're averaging 40 boats a day now," Kevin says, picking up binoculars. "We'll have about 1,700 this month total. I've got one, two, three, four, five . . . ." He raises the binoculars. "Six, seven, eight, nine that I can see coming right now."

The drawbridge really is just a 480-ton Lazy Susan, 170 feet of steel and asphalt on a turntable. It makes a 90-degree turn, opening two water lanes between heavy wood pilings. Built in 1960, before electronics became so advanced and condensed, the bridge employs technology developed half a century ago. A big console and a cumbersome bank of electronic relays swing it open and shut.

"If this panel were built today, it probably would be about that size," Kevin says, indicating a small box. "It's relatively simple to operate. It looks more complicated than it is. The hard part is learning wind conditions and things like that."

Wind today: steady out of the north-northeast at 25, occasionally gusting to 30. The murky brown water of the river and Albemarle Sound just north of the bridge froths with whitecaps.

"Mouth of the Alligator is notorious for rough water," Kevin says. "It's one of the roughest places on the Intracoastal Waterway. When the wind comes out of the north or northeast, it blows across the sound and when it hits this river, it's just like a funnel. It's just a rough place to be. October a year ago, we had a bad blow. Boats were coming up even with the bridge."

At times the wind blows hard enough to put the bridge out of commission.

"Like today I'm having to give it a lot of power to get it open, and to close it, I just let the wind do it."

31

Kevin Roughton on Alligator Bridge

Kevin is 27, a short, stocky man with curly hair and eyes that smile over a walrus mustache. He became a bridge tender when he finished high school in Columbia, 12 miles west of the bridge. He worked only three months before enrolling at East Carolina University.

He quit college after a year and a half to play music. He'd started taking guitar lessons at 8, was playing in bands by the time he was 13. His ambition was to be a professional musician, but after two hard years on the road, he went back to bridge tending, this time on a nearby bridge over Albemarle Sound.

He worked that job two years before music pulled him back in 1980. Another year on the road left him broke and discouraged, and he returned again to Alligator Bridge, as the tenders and boat captains call Warren Bridge.

After five months, he was laid off, and during that time he began performing solo at clubs and restaurants on Outer Banks beaches, playing guitar and singing, his repertoire ranging from country to classical. Later that year he was called back to work at the bridge, this time as relief man.

"My main gig is playing," he says. "That's my work. I've got the sickness. It's a disease. But I'm satisfied to play and share my talent. I'm not chasing dreams of stardom. I consider myself a success in doing that. I've touched a lot of people through my music. The main reason I'm a bridge tender is because I'm a musician first."

The job gives him steady income, time to perform and usually—when the yachts aren't migrating—plenty of time to practice. But today he's hardly had time to touch his guitar.

He keeps opening and closing the bridge, rarely for single boats, usually for two, three, four, the smaller ones following in the protective wakes of bigger ones in the rough water. Three bearing feminine names—the Fran-Tastic, the Mary E, the Miss Gina, all from Wilmington, Del., pass in line. Kevin enters each in the log, along with time of passing, weather conditions, length of time the bridge was open, number of highway vehicles held up.

He delays one impatient, horn-honking yachtsman briefly because a single car is on the bridge. "I really hate to drop the gates on somebody like this car," he says. "I just think it's dangerous."

Another boat he holds up so a trailing boat can catch up. "I try to bunch 'em up if I can," he says, entering the two in his log. "I've already had 31 today." He started work at 8 a.m. It is now 1:20 p.m.

"You're going to have to let me play for you before you go," he says. He likes to play for any visitor who stops by. A couple of times he has played for hapless motorists whose cars broke down on the bridge.

But before he can reach for his guitar, the National Weather Service calls for his regular report on conditions. And the captain of the tug Rolita, somewhere south, radios to ask him to make some telephone calls, a common request for the bridge tenders.

The calls completed, Kevin finally puts a cloth over the bib of his Red Camel overalls so the metal buttons won't scratch his guitar and sits to play. It is a beautiful piece, and as he plays, a big timber truck roars past, providing an unneeded bass, vibrating the whole bridge.

"Oh, that's just a piece I wrote," Kevin says when he finishes. "It doesn't even have a name."

Through the windows to the south, a tug can be seen approaching, pushing a military landing craft, followed by several yachts. "Gotta get to work," he says, propping his guitar on a stand. He grins. "Hey, listen, encourage people to stop—just to say hello. Maytag repairmen are not the loneliest people in town."

Isolation

COLUMBIA   At the Alligator River, Tyrrell County and desolation begin. The highway runs for miles with no sign of civilization other than the straight, flat strip of road and the dark, brooding canal alongside that resulted from the highway's construction.

But beyond the trees and wild growth that line the roadway, huge earthmoving machines can be heard at work, digging miles of drainage canals, clearing thousands of acres for huge farms, leaving miniature mountains of forest debris smoking in their wake.

Tyrrell is North Carolina's most sparsely populated county, with only 4,000 people on its 583 square miles of swamps, peat bogs and farm fields. Forty percent of its people live under the poverty level. In only one county, Bertie, is the percentage higher.

The county's only town, Columbia, has only one sit-down restaurant, the Scuppernong, its restrooms labeled with silhouettes of hunting dogs, one marked "pointers," the other "setters." There is no movie theater.

With its isolation and slim prospects for the future, Tyrrell has had trouble holding onto its ambitious young people—and, in recent years, its doctors.

For 30 years, Tyrrell's only doctor was S.C. Chaplin, a Wake Forest graduate who came to Columbia in 1922. Doc Chaplin, as he was called, opened the county's first hospital in his home in 1924 and a few years later started building a small hospital on Broad Street. As the hospital grew into a rambling white building. Doc became so greatly beloved that his penchant for driving fast in his Star automobile was overlooked.

But after Doc fell dead of a heart attack at 56 in 1952, killed, everybody said, by overwork, Tyrrell had a succession of doctors. Doc Chaplin's hospital fell into disrepair and eventually into disuse. It became harder and harder to get a reliable doctor to work in the county.

In 1979, a group of citizens got together to do something about that. They wanted to get a U.S. Public Health Service doctor and clinic. When their proposal was approved but no money allocated for the clinic, the group set about raising the money. After they got $11,000, the state kicked in $40,000. With the clinic ready, the U.S. government sent a doctor to Tyrrell.

Dave Denekas arrived in July 1981 and was greeted by 50 thankful people who took him out to dinner, not at the Scuppernong but several miles up the road in Washington County at Miss Donnie's, where the restrooms are marked less cutely.

Dave was 28 then, a native of Chicago who'd always lived in cities, a graduate of Brown University and Stanford Medical School. He'd just completed his residency at George Washington University Hospital in Washington. In exchange for his agreement to serve two years in an isolated spot, the U.S. government paid for two years of his medical training.

He might have been sent to serve Indians in the West or Eskimos in Alaska, but when he learned his assignment was the South, he picked North Carolina because it was as close as he could get to friends and pleasures in Washington. He chose Columbia over several other areas in the state—including more appealing Hatteras and Ocracoke—because he wanted the challenge of starting a new clinic.

"I came expecting there would be a lot of farmers happily dancing around their John Deere tractors," he says with a smile, "that there would be no pressure. But there's just as much pressure here as anywhere. It's isolation and loneliness and poverty that cause the pressures here."

The people and their medical problems, Dave soon discovered, were little different than he had encountered in the city. But life for him was quite different.

He bought an old house near the clinic that needed a lot of work. He was working on it one day when a boy stopped to watch and started talking.

"I said, 'Come in and eat lunch,'" Dave recalls, "and he said, 'OK,' and he did. He came back next day and said, 'Can I eat lunch with you?' Pretty soon there were five."

The children, who lived nearby, were fatherless and had a mother who paid them little attention.

"They were pretty sad," says Dave, who isn't married. "They adopted me."

When their mother finally moved to Delaware and took them away, Dave had mixed feelings.

"Like watching your mother-in-law go over the cliff in your Cadillac," he says. "They were more than I could handle."

A 27-foot sailboat and occasional trips to Washington allowed him to escape the isolation he often felt, but there were many things he missed, paramount among them symphonies, Chinese restaurants and shoptalk with other doctors. Still, when the end of his two years of obligated service came up last July, Dave elected to stay in Columbia.

"I could see the clinic wasn't doing well enough for me to leave," he says.

The clinic is a small brick building behind Dr. Chaplin's old hospital. Three other people work there. Only one, Shirley Blount, a clinical assistant who'd worked for the town's last doctor, is a native of the area. Debbie Spear, receptionist and record keeper, came three years ago after her father read about the area's rich soil and sold his Ohio farm to buy some of it. She has since married a local fellow and settled to stay.

"Back home it was just rush, rush, rush," she says. "Here, it's slow and friendly and everybody moves at their own pace."

Angela Martin, who arrived in January, is the staff's newest member. She is a nurse practitioner, licensed to treat certain illnesses and injuries without supervision by a doctor. Unlike the first nurse practitioner at the clinic, who left after her Public Health Service assignment was finished, Angela came because she wanted to.

A native of Rockingham County who grew up near Reidsville and graduated from nursing school at the University of North Carolina at Greensboro, Angela worked awhile in Raleigh before going back to school at the university in Chapel Hill and getting her master's degree in 1983. She was working at the Caswell County Health Department in Yanceyville when she read about the job opening in Columbia and applied for it.

"I was basically bored," she says. "I wanted to go somewhere people really need me. I wanted to go somewhere I could learn a lot. I've learned more since I've been here than I learned the whole time in school."

This is the first day after a holiday weekend, and before the clinic opens Dave predicts it will be a busy day. The morning bears him out. The waiting room remains full. It is the regular run of ailments, but shortly before noon a call for help comes from a house nearby.

Dave sprints down the street to find a 77-year-old man suffering congestive heart failure. He summons an ambulance. Back at the clinic, Dave works in the back of the ambulance to stabilize the man. Serious cases must go to the hospital at Edenton, 30 miles away, or Greenville, much farther. Dave decides the man should go to Edenton and leaves in the ambulance with him.

"Is he doing OK?" Angela asks a student nurse who had been helping the doctor.

"He looks pretty bad," she says.

Angela is taking a break, talking about this area where she has chosen to live and work. She and her husband, Dale, a construction worker and cabinet maker, also from near Reidsville, made the decision together. They like to sail and they wanted to live in a small town on the coast, where they could sail and rear their 18-month-old daughter, Melissa, away from city pressures. They rented a small blue Cape Cod house near the clinic and have been so happy so far that they hope to stay forever.

"I really love walking to work," Angela says. "When I was in Raleigh, I just got real tired of driving on interstates and 5 o'clock traffic. I can walk to the dry cleaners, walk to get groceries. I can ride my bike anywhere. That's probably the greatest pleasure of all, not having to rush to get anywhere.

"Sometimes I wish this area had a little more to offer, but then I think about some of the disadvantages of the city. I guess there's no perfect place to raise children. I think a lot about Melissa growing up here. What if she wants to be a musician or something? She probably couldn't do it here. She couldn't get the training. But you have to decide what's important."

Ironically, it is music that has played a crucial role in Dave's decision to leave the clinic to take an emergency room job in a hospital near Washington.

"See, I'm a cello player of sorts," he says. "Down here, there's not much call for it."

The clinic is doing much better now. This year it should be able to repay more than $40,000 to the federal government. Dave thinks it will someday be self-sustaining and attract a doctor who wants to make a private practice, the clinic's goal. But until then the Public Health Service has assigned a new doctor, now finishing his residency in Chapel Hill.

Dave returns to the clinic in early afternoon to face a backlog of waiting patients. At 4:40, 20 minutes before the clinic's normal closing time, eight people are still in the waiting room. Dave opens the door and spots a hulking youth.

"You aren't a football physical already are you?" he asks.

The young man nods. "There's some more coming behind me," he says.

Dave slaps himself in the forehead. "Somebody hit me over the head with a brick," he says.

Passage

West of Columbia, the land opens into broad, flat fields, dark and rich, carved from the forest and drained by ditches. Some of the fields reach for miles to faint treelines on distant horizons.

Potatoes grow here in spring, corn and peanuts in summer, wheat in winter.

Tractors working the far fields can be distinguished only by the dust clouds they stir. They are huge, these tractors, many enclosed with air-conditioned cabs, some outfitted with stereo and CB radios that connect them to home and one another. When they take to the highway, as they frequently do, oftentimes pulling implements broad enough to block both lanes, they sometimes bring traffic to a crawl.

The houses cling to the highway. They are for the most part modest in size. The newer ones are porchless, built of brick, roofed with asphalt shingles that cover carports, obviously occupied by people who value cars and pickup trucks more than the pleasures of porches. The older houses are of wood, painted white and roofed with tin. They all have porches where in the heat of day and coolness of early evening, people can be seen sitting in swings and rockers, watching the passing traffic.

Old and new, almost every house has a vegetable garden, some big enough to feed several families. Near older houses, small family cemeteries can sometimes be seen on the edges—and now and then in the middle—of plowed fields.

Seven miles out of Columbia, the highway passes from Tyrrell into Washington County, and two miles later, bypasses Creswell's old downtown.

On the western edge of town, huge grain elevators stand abandoned in weeds, out of business, a big sign proclaiming their availability. But a nearby farmer is prosperous enough to possess not only a big brick house but a swimming pool and tennis court as well. Down the road, a sign on the mailbox of another big brick house proclaims this the home of the county's top broiler producer of 1983.

A fire tower, second in the highway's first 50 miles, looms in the middle of a state-owned complex harboring forest service offices, bridge and highway maintenance shops and the Washington County prison unit, where a basketball game is under way beyond the high fence topped with razor wire.

Moving northwestward now, the highway passes cattle grazing in pastures tinged yellow by tiny wildflowers, and through a bog where a few cypress tress stand protected by highway right-of-way from the fate that befell their closeby neighbors, now graying stumps sawed close to the muck.

Soon the highway takes its closest swipe at Albemarle Sound, which remains invisible beyond plowed fields, the only evidence of it being an incongruous string of expensive waterfront homes looking as if they are perched on the edge of space.

At Pleasant Grove—an intersection, a church, three stores—the highway swings briefly southward toward Roper. A mile outside the town, a pungent odor fills the air, different from the aromas of fertilizer, hog parlors and chicken houses that have perfumed the air so far. An unfamiliar crop presents itself. The leafy plants with multiple spikes budding white, some already beginning to flower lavender, cover acres.

"Sage," says Billy Edwards, who's tinkering with a John Deere tractor in a fenced lot beside his brick house across the road from the crop.

"The kind that goes in sausage?"

"Naw, they use it for perfume and oil."

It has been grown in the county for about five years, he says, but never by him. He grows corn and peanuts.

"R.J. Reynolds handles it," he says.

This crop, he says, part of some 800 acres grown in the county, is about three weeks from harvest.

"They just cut the flowers. That's all they want. It gets right purplish. That's some stinkin' damn stuff when it starts to flower. I never smelled nothin' like it."

Roper presents back doors to the highway as it skirts Main Street by less than a block, heading westward toward Plymouth, eight miles away. Other crops occupy some fields now. Cabbages being harvested by crews. Young watermelon vines not yet sprawling.

As Plymouth comes closer, the trucks become more frequent, behemoths laboring under loads of massive tree trunks stacked high, converging on the highway from many directions, creating logjams in the traffic flow. At Plymouth, they turn northward onto Ken Trowbridge Road, where, hulking beyond the trees, too big to hide, a monster waits. At the tree-eating, river-slurping, smoke belching Weyerhauser pulp plant, whose voracious appetite is insatiable, their loads are snatched away by a single claw and fed into the maw that provides sustenance for people from several counties around.

By-Passed By Time

CRESWELL   Drive into downtown Creswell and drive back 85 years in time. Main Street bears the look of an old western town with its two-story wooden buildings roofed with tin, little changed since the turn of the century except for the saggings and grayings of age.

The soda shop is the oldest business in town. Model airplanes fill the front window, and a bumper sticker on the glass advises, "When guns are outlawed only outlaws will have guns."

This is an authentic old-timey soda shop where cherry Cokes are made from syrup, fruit is squeezed on the spot for orangeades and lemonades, and milkshakes are hand-dipped, mixed thick in steel cups, 24 ounces for 85 cents.

Nobody in Creswell finds the big display of firearms, ammunition and hunting supplies at the end of the fountain incongruous (this is, after all, hunting country). Neither do they find it strange that the lemonades and cherry Cokes are made by a man wearing a pistol.

There is nothing ominous about the pistol. It only indicates that Walter Peal, the owner, also is chief deputy for the Washington County Sheriff's Department, a job he's had for 27 years.

It was Walter's late father, also Walter, a sheriff's deputy himself for 38 years (when the county had only two deputies), who started the soda shop in the 1920s. Walter, who's 58, grew up in the shop.

"Didn't have no running water around here," he says. "Only water we had was an artesian well, 410 feet deep. Supplied the people of this town for I reckon 40 years. I used to have to tote water from the well to the soda shop and store it upstairs in barrels. That's the only way it would run down to the soda shop."

Walter is seated in one of two booths in the red and blue soda shop, reminiscing about the town with his friend of many years, Elwood Davenport, nicknamed Herman, who's 67. Both have spent their whole lives in Creswell.

"Used to be old gas pumps out on the street," Walter says. "You come into this town and there'd be mules, horses and carts tied up."

"Just like an ol' western town," Elwood says.

"Just on this Main Street back when I was a kid, there was nine bootleggers, just on this street," Walter goes on. "Election day in this town used to be something."

"Good times. Good times, I mean. Yessir," adds Elwood.

"There was more people turned out and more free likker handed out," Walter says, "and this last election it was just like a funeral. I

Elwood Davenport, left, Walter Peal

reckon this town has changed, just like everybody else."

Outside Walter and Elwood point out some of the change. The old town well is gone, the pipes rusted out years ago. But when it failed another well was drilled nearby, this one 394 feet deep, and it put out a steady stream of water until the phosphate pits were opened at Aurora years ago. Then the water level dropped and the town had to put a hand pump on the well, which remains in service. The water from the well tastes heavily of sulphur, but some people prefer it and think it has special properties.

"People come here from Virginia, they come from South Carolina, they come from everywhere to get that water," Walter says.

Businesses are still thriving in some of Creswell's old buildings, but others stand vacant now. Walter and Elwood still see the buildings as they were. They can name what and who was in every one.

"That used to be the ol' butcher shop on the corner," Elwood says. "Then Mr. Pritchett moved in there with the hardware store."

"Ol' country store there," Walter says, pointing out another building. "Harry Walker used to own that. God Awmighty, he had anything in the world you wanted in there. That was a second Sears & Roebuck."

They go on pointing and naming until Walter says, "There's just not much left, but we're going to keep it going, ain't we, Herman?"

"That's the truth," Elwood says. "Yessir."

At the head of Main Street sits another graying building where C.N. Davenport opened a blacksmith shop not long after the turn of the century. By the '20s the shop had evolved into a combination machine shop, garage, gas station, grocery and funeral home.

"My father had a slogan," says C.N. Davenport Jr., who has been called Mike since high school days. "He put it on his letterhead and his calendar: 'We feed the living, bury the dead, make your auto go ahead.' Yeah, we made our own coffins, buried 'em for $50."

Mike will be 86 this summer, making him one of Creswell's oldest citizens. He grew up in his father's businesses and took them over after his death in 1946. The funeral business he gave up in 1948, and later he dropped groceries. It was the machine shop that held Mike's interest.

"I done a lot with metal," he says. "What needed to be done, I'd do it. Farming equipment was my main business, keeping up the farmers. See, this is a farming area. If it wasn't for the farmers here, wouldn't be no town."

For 10 years Mike served on the town council; and in 1953, five years after Creswell got its first paved street, he became mayor. He remained in office 20 years before stepping down.

In 1965, when he was 67, Mike gave up his machine shop and retired. That same year, he moved out of the old family home next to the shop and into a modern new brick house he built nearby. His wife of 48 years, Gladys, died in 1979.

"I lost my wife and all my fishing buddies, all in 18 months," he says.

His three children all live in other states, two in far-off California, and Mike doesn't see as many people or feel as much a part of things as he once did. But he keeps busy with the fire department he helped organize, the Rotary Club, the Masons, the Methodist Church; and he spends a lot of time puttering in a little shop behind his house.

There he shows off pictures of a device he perfected and built with a Hungarian inventor years ago when loggers had to skid logs onto trucks. The device allowed a tractor to lift the logs. It was produced by an Ohio company, but other equipment came along to do the same job and few were ever sold. Mike is proud of it, nevertheless, just as he is proud of getting a water system for the town while he was mayor, along with a new school and post office.

But for these accomplishments he has received little recognition. Another has brought him far more. It is in his back yard, enclosed in plastic panels and Plexiglass—a full-sized orange tree that he planted in 1965 and has carefully nurtured since, warming it in winter with gas and electric heaters that set off warning lights if they fail.

"Year before last, I had a thousand oranges off of it," Mike says. "I spent more money on that tree than a little, but I meet a lot of folks now say, 'Hey, you're the orange man.' That stuff gets out on you because it's unusual, I guess."

Love and Libraries

ROPER   Coincidence brought them together. He was city-bred, a boatswain's mate in the Navy. She was a fifth-grade teacher in a country town.

He was escorting a group of younger sailors from Norfolk to New York, where they would board a new ship for the war in Europe. She was taking her niece to New York for the first time to visit relatives.

They came together on the old ferry that ran to Cape Charles. He saw that his sailors were talking and laughing with the young woman, and went to inquire of the older woman if the sailors were being a nuisance. Not at all, she said, and they stuck up a conversation.

Both were impressed. He thought she was smart and such a lady. She thought him handsome, considerate and quite a gentleman.

Her name was Daisy Lee Clark, his Vernon Williams. When they learned they all were on the way to New York, they agreed to keep company on the train. He and she talked all the way, and by the time they reached the city, they'd exchanged addresses and agreed to correspond.

More than a year later, he wrote and told her his ship was on the way home.

"I knew it was love," he says with a smile, "because when my ship pulled into New York, she was there. 'Bell Bottom Sailor, Suits of Navy Blue,' that was her song."

They married in 1946 after he was discharged. He had thought about going back home to New Brunswick, N.J., to find a job, but she wanted to return to her students in Roper. He came not knowing what to expect except that her brother had assured him a job in a garage.

Not long after they arrived, they bought a house and small store on U.S. 64 east of town at the intersection of a sandy road called Backwoods. They bought the property from whites and their neighbors on each side were white, but nobody objected. Vernon soon learned that a storekeeper's life was not an easy one. Most of his customers wanted credit; some paid and some didn't.

He decided he'd have to do something different, so in 1948 he applied for a beer license and became the first black in the area to get one. He took out most of the grocery shelves, turned a counter into a bar at the back, bought a flashy jukebox, added some benches and a couple of rickety tables, put a sign on the wall that said, 'Leave All Cursing Outside, Please,' and another that said, 'Credit Makes

44

Daisy and Vernon Williams

Enemies, Let's Be Friends,' and the little store became a lively spot
at nighttime.

"It was a new item here and we made some money, too," Vernon
says.

It was not without drawbacks, though. Bootleg joints not far away
were scenes of fights, cuttings, shootings, and some of those people
were drawn to Williams' Place, as it was called. But they had Vernon
to deal with.

"They knew I didn't take no foolishness, that's all," he says. "I
told 'em, 'When you come in here, you better be right.' I just didn't
allow it."

Such was the reputation of the place than an unusual thing happened.

"After we got the jukebox," says Daisy, "the older people around here wanted a special hour to come and hear religious music. So we got some religious records and set up a special hour from 4 to 5 on Sunday."

"Didn't sell any beer that hour," says Vernon.

"If anybody came wanting beer, he'd say, 'You just have to wait an hour,'" remembers Daisy.

"Nobody around here had any place to go," says Vernon. "They'd all come—in carts and wagons and everything. Even the bootleggers. Some of the biggest bootleggers, they'd come, bring their whole families, set and listen to the music."

"I tell you the truth, I think we had more whites than blacks," says Daisy. "My dentist right now, he was raised out this road and his father used to bring him up here. I made him spell. I'd say, 'Spell secretary for me.' He always got all those letters jumbled up. When I had to have some dental work done last summer, he said, 'One thing's sure, I won't ever forget how to spell secretary.'"

The business placed difficult demands on both of them.

"The hours were awful," says Daisy, who had to get up early to teach. "I couldn't go to sleep until he got in the house."

"To make the money," says Vernon, "you had to stay with the folks. As long as they stayed, I stayed. Sometimes, it would be 3 or 4 o'clock in the morning."

That was part of the reason that in the early '50s Vernon went off to Raleigh to attend barber school. He returned and opened a two-chair shop in a storeroom of his place. But barbering alone was not enough, he discovered, so he had two jobs.

Daisy wasn't satisfied either. She was dedicated to education and she wanted more of it for herself. She had been one of 10 children and her father had given up farming and taken a railroad job because he wanted all of his children to get an education. All 10 finished high school, but Daisy was the only one to go on to college.

"My father said, 'Wumps, I want you to promise me you'll go to school,'" Daisy remembers. "I wanted to make him happy."

Shortly after Vernon finished barber training, Daisy started spending summers in New York, studying for her master's degree in education at Columbia University. She got it in 1957, but by then her interests had turned to libraries. So three years later, she started returning to New York each summer, and in 1968 she got a second master's degree in library science. She even earned 19 hours toward a doctorate, but she was too busy starting libraries in schools at home to finish it.

Daisy retired in 1974 after having established libraries in three different schools, and Vernon is all but retired. He still cuts a little hair, but mostly for old-timers. "Since that Afro thing, there's not much business," he says. "You've seen all that hair on their heads.

I don't mess with that stuff." He has kept the store open, although he doesn't stay in it much anymore. The jukebox has been broken for more than a year.

"Maybe some Friday nights some of the fellows will come by and have a beer," he says.

Daisy wasn't one to be idle in retirement. For years she'd been upset that Roper had no public library, so she started organizing people, blacks and whites, prominent people and not so prominent, and now the town has a library with some 12,000 volumes in the old Baptist Church. Daisy works there four hours a day as a volunteer and organizes many programs for children, all of whom quickly learn to spell secretary.

Recently, the people of Roper did some organizing in Daisy's behalf. They held a surprise dinner to honor her at a restaurant in Plymouth. The governor gave her an award for volunteerism.

Other than that she could not bear children, Daisy has no regrets about the way life has gone for her and Vernon, but there are times when she feels she may have deprived her husband by asking him to come to such an isolated spot to live, so far away from his home and the life he had known.

"To me now," says Vernon, "she often says, 'I know sometimes you want to go back to your home and live,' and I say, 'Hunh-huh. No. This is my home now. I love this place.'"

High Water

JAMESVILLE   Ed Roberson was feeding his crickets. They chirped softly in the big topless box and crawled over every inch of the walls except for the painted band around the top.

"That white paint, it's slick; they can't climb on it," Ed said, explaining why the crickets stay in the box.

Why don't they jump out?

"Ain't got sense enough." He turned his wheelchair contemptuously away from the box. "They could fly out if they wanted to."

It was late afternoon at Roberson's Marina in what should have been one of the best months of the year, but it had been another lousy day in a month that was remaining disastrous.

"I sold a half a tube of crickets and one float," he said. "A 30-cent float. Uh, Lord, I don't know whether I've sold a half a case of sody pops or not."

It had been only 10 days earlier that Ed finally had been able to get back into the small concrete block building where he sells snacks, bait and fishing supplies.

"We had about 12 inches of water in the building for three months. That water started coming up the first of February. We had the neighborhood come in and jack the boxes up, ol' counters and mess. Ol' silt settled on the floor. It was about three inches deep when we started with the water hoses washing the silt out of here. Just brooms and water hoses, all you can do with it. Scrub and brush, scrub and brush, all you can do with it.

"See the water line here. I been expecting the building to fall down, all this water."

This building was built 20 years ago by Ed's father, Lelon, to replace a rickety wooden shack that once had stood in its place. He built it only a few feet from Gardner's Creek, a picturesque stream, dark with tannic acid, that would qualify as a river anywhere else. It rises in the Diamond City Dismal Swamp and follows a meandering course to a water maze called Devil's Gut before emptying into the Roanoke River. It is one of the most inviting spots along U.S. 64, an irresistible lure to fishermen.

Fishing camps have stood on this spot by the highway for as long as anybody in the area can remember. Ed's great-granddaddy, granddaddy and daddy all hunted, trapped and fished along the creek and brought their catches to this spot to clean them. Ed's daddy, who died in 1968, bought the place in 1932 and built a small white house by the road up the hill from the creek. His daddy made

Ed Roberson

a living here serving fishermen in spring, summer and fall, trapping in winter.

"At one time, my daddy had I reckon 20 boats he rented. I think he got something like 50 cents a day. Now this was years back. But no more. You couldn't think about renting out a boat with a motor on it. There's two or three ol' pieces of boat out there, but you don't hardly ever rent a boat now."

"You can't make a living at it now, no sir, not really. Used to you could, but it's got to where it's getting shorter each year when the fish will bite. I don't know whether it's because there's not as many fish or because there's so many fishin'.

"Lot of people claim Weyerhauser pollutes the river so fish can't survive, but I don't think so. They got all those settlin' lakes. Whenever they drop that water back in Roanoke River, I'm sure it's better tastin' than a lot of city water."

A lot of fish have come from the creek, and Ed has snapshots to prove it. Big striped bass, called rockfish hereabouts. Lunker large-mouth bass. Long stringers of bream and catfish. He rattled off weights, names and towns of people who caught them as he showed them off.

Once, Ed did a lot of fishing himself. No more.

"I get in a boat now and set out there two or three hours, and it takes me three or four days to get over it. I got in an automobile wreck when I was young and here lately I've been having a lot of trouble with my bones. June the ninth, 1953. I was 16 years old, riding with a boy from Greenville. He was actin' like a fool, runnin' too fast and turned over. Tore me up. Back broke in three places. Paralyzed. I spent about as much time in the hospital since then as I have out.

"After I first got hurt, I'd go fishin' every day. Just can't fish anymore. 'Course when the water's three months over the banks, there's not much fishin' you can do.

"Worst problem in the world's our water situation. A few years ago, Kerr Reservoir started filling up and they said flooding on the Roanoke would be improved. If anything, it's worse. Now in spring there's thousands and thousands of acres under water and they can't farm 'em at all.

"Herring used to run up here. This year they didn't do anything. I sell these special device fishing licenses for dipping herring. I should've sold 200 this spring. I sold six. Wasn't a herring caught here this year. High water. Nobody didn't fish. It's been a sorry, sorry spring because of this water, I tell you."

He looked out the open back door at the water only a few feet away.

"If this water stays like it is right now, it'll be sorry tomorrow, too. High and muddy. That water when I came in here this morning was black. Now it's right milky. That's local rainwater, and now they're sayin' there's going to be another big rain. It's liable to be right back in the building."

No. 90 Station

WILLIAMSTON   Pauline Goddard rousts herself from the couch where she is resting. She had been to the doctor earlier in the day, and she still isn't feeling well.

"You name it, I got it, I think," she says. "I've tried every doctor and I finally wound up with a chirypractor doctor this morning."

A nearby table top, covered with medicine vials, is testament to her quest for relief.

"I got asthma, emphysema, something," she says, lighting an L&M.

Across the room, her mother, Sadie Davis, white-haired and 91 years old, sits in a reclining chair, covered with a sheet against the stirrings of the overhead fan, her remaining foot propped on pillows. She lost the other foot and part of her leg two months ago to poor circulation. An infection that set in after the operation still has not been quelled completely.

"I don't know what to tell you," says Pauline, who is 69. "I'm not too good with dates and things. All I know is when this highway was put through here, this was the first and only station between Williamston and Jamesville. Is that right, Mama? You're older than I am."

Sadie remains silent.

No. 90 Station. It sits next door to Pauline's brick house. She worked there for 42 years and still owns it. It is the oldest gas station in these parts, surely one of the oldest in the state. It has been an outlet for Texaco gas for 60 years, in business even before U.S. 64 was created in 1933—so old that it still bears the name of the old road, Route 90.

Gothee and Golden Goddard, bachelor brothers, uncles to Pauline's husband, Grady, built the station in 1924, the year route 90 was paved. They had another little store on a nearby curve that was being bypassed by the highway, so they built the new place. It was a fancy station for the time with a roof that reached out to cover the hand-operated gas pumps.

The Goddard brothers operated it several years, then rented it to another fellow. Eventually, they sold it to the oil company that supplied their gas. Grady and Pauline rented it from the oil company for several years before buying it. Pauline isn't sure about any of these dates.

"You remember what year Miss Lily Roberson died?" she asks her mother, trying to recall one of them.

"No. I remember the winter very well, but I don't remember the year," Sadie says.

Pauline Goddard

"I be derned if I know," Pauline says after trying to remember when she and Grady bought the place. "I'd have to look up some old records."

"That year after you married, wasn't it?" says her mother.

"What Mama?"

"The year after you married."

"No, we bought it the year that Golden died."

Pauline finally decides on 1937, the year after their marriage, as the year she and Grady started renting the place, sometime in the '40s that they bought the station. But she has no trouble remembering the long days she spent there—or the good times.

"From anytime you got up till anytime the crowd let you go to bed," she says. "That's the best I can tell you. From sunrise till bedtime. We got out there early and we stayed till they all left.

"Everybody gathered out there. They would have big deer hunts and they'd gather out there and talk about it. They'd kill the deer and bring 'em there to dress 'em.

"They'd set out there at night and play Rook. We never had any gambling. Just play cards. Rook mostly. Not much Setback, if any."

"Can you still play that, Mammy?" one of Pauline's granddaughters, who has been listening to her reminiscences, asks her great-grandmother.

"I can't do nothin' no more," says Sadie.

"As far as I know we were the first ones to have a television around here, anywhere that I know of," Pauline goes on. "It was an Emerson, and I still got it. I'd like to have it fixed up. Just for a keepsake. Couldn't get nothin' on it but Norfolk then, and it looked like a big snow between you and everybody you were looking at."

As time went on, television became clearer, but the station became less a gathering place. Still, it held on. After Grady died ("I don't know what year he died," says Pauline. "You'll have to ask somebody that can remember better than I can. He's been dead 14 years, I think."), Pauline continued operating it herself. She quit six years ago.

"I got tired of it," she says. "It was more than I could do. Night and day. I couldn't take it."

Her daughter, Brenda Davis, operates it now. Pauline insists on only one thing: that the name remain unchanged, a memorial to another time.

"I don't never want it changed," she says. "Nobody said nothing about changing it until we got it, and then I said. 'Don't change it.' I liked the name. This is the only place that's been on this road all that time. That's why I don't want it changed."

Passage

West of Williamston, towns come in quick succession, only a few miles apart—Everetts, Robersonville, Parmele. . . .

Everetts has two claims to fame. It is the town that provided the lumber for the original boardwalk in Atlantic City, and in 1927 it was the site of a baseball game between a town team and the local school team that went for 54 innings and was called because of darkness with the score tied at 100.

In those days, Everetts was an industrious place with a lumber mill, cotton gin, feed mill and a thriving downtown that included several stores, a bank and an auto dealership that sold Champions, Stars, Durants, Essexes and Hudsons. At one time it also had a plant that bottled Zimba Cola and Guth Cola.

Henry Leman Barnhill, better known as H.L., owned the bottling company, which went out of business in 1947.

"The main reason it closed up, I was in the tobacco business and I just didn't have time to put in it," says H.L. "Course, if I'd been making a million dollars at it, I wouldn't've closed it up."

H.L. owns every building in downtown Everetts except the post office and one other. But only one business besides the post office survives. That's Barnhill Supply Co., the "Everything for Everybody" store, founded in 1896. H.L. owns it, too.

He sits now in the store office under the stern portrait visages of his father, Julius T. Barnhill, who founded the business, and his older brother, J.T. Jr., who took over after his father's death and ran it until his own death in 1972.

H.L. never had much taste for the store business. His father helped him buy a tobacco warehouse in Williamston when he was a young man, and he stayed in that business 52 years (he still owns the warehouse but leases it) and loved it.

"Nobody ever been in the tobacco business what didn't enjoy it," he says. "Most of 'em that got out died out."

But the family business—or what was left of it—fell to him after his brother's death, and he feels an obligation to keep it going. "There's not 25 percent of the business done here now that there was in the '20s and in the '40s," he says. "Before the Depression, when this town was lively, like most little towns were at that time, my daddy had eight employees in this building."

Now there are three: two longtime employees who operate it and a bookkeeper.

"I just come down here twice a day, in the morning and afternoon,

H.L. Barnhill in downtown Everetts

to see if the rest of 'em are doing anything," H.L. says.

H.L. soon will be 80, and he doesn't know what will become of the business after he is gone. "I haven't got any children so I haven't got anybody to take over. I'm afraid when I'm gone there won't be nothin' left."

Outside, H.L. looks at the closed-up, decaying brick buildings that he owns—what used to be downtown Everetts—and contemplates their future.

"Anything you consider home, you hate to see it go down if you've got a little pride and feeling about it," he says, "but I expect they'll just stay here and fall down, like a lot of other little towns."

At the Bus Station Grill in Robersonville, Mildred McArthur is having lunch. Her grandson, Bart Greene, owns the combination bus station, convenience store, grill and beer hall, and it is a busy place. Electronic games set up a cacophony around her as a group of locals laughs and drinks beer nearby.

"This used to be, they called it the town that never slept, because it was such a lively little town," Mildred says. "The young people just had a big time here. Dances over at the warehouse. They used to say it was a jumpin' and jivin' place, all that crowd I knew, my people. They're too old for that now. I don't know what the young people do now."

Mildred came to Robersonville in 1947, two years after her husband, Stuart, had bought an interest in a feed business in the town.

"They didn't want any newcomers in this little town," she says. "I had to live in Rocky Mount for almost two years before we could find a place to live. I tell you, newcomers have a hard time. When my husband came here, the Methodist preacher told him, 'You won't be here but a year. Nobody stays but six months to a year.'"

But the McArthurs stayed and opened the FCX, which they still operate. Now they are fixtures in the town.

"I think if people do live here and stay a year, they love it," Mildred says. "I don't know, it's just something about it. Seems like once you get established here, you don't want to leave. It was quite a change to come to a little town like this, but once we got situated, I love it. It's home to me."

Parmele was once a confusion of railroad tracks. Tracks converged on the community from five different directions.

"Sunday afternoon there'd be about five passenger trains up here and all the people would come, there'd be the biggest crowd of people—to see the trains, don't you know," says Blanche Roberson. "Down there in the railroad office in Jacksonville, Florida, Parmele was a great thing on the map. All these railroads coming in here. But Lord, things is changed now."

It's been nearly 40 years since a passenger train last passed through Parmele, and many of the freight trains also have been discontinued.

"We only have trains now from Rocky Mount to Plymouth and Rocky Mount to Greenville. That's the only ones we have. They've took up the tracks, took up the switches, everything."

The tracks that once passed by the front door of Blanche's big two-story house were ripped up last year, leaving only the bed on a big embankment. "I didn't care," she says. "Didn't make no difference to me. I don't never see the trains."

Blanche's husband was a railroad man. Nicholas Roberson moved to Parmele from Williamston and went to work for the railroad as a brakeman in 1919 after serving in World War I. Blanche, who has lived in the town all her life, married him four years later. In 1946, they bought the big house that once had been the roadmaster's house. At the front door stood a huge coal chute to which the steam engines backed to replenish their fuel supplies. It was a noisy, dusty place to live, but it didn't bother Blanche and Nicholas. They were railroad people.

Nicholas died of a blood clot in 1949, before the arrival in Parmele of diesel engines, which he'd predicted he'd never see.

"He worked the day he died," Blanche says.

Lots of railroad people lived in the town in those days. Blanche reels off names. "Hugh Spaight, Tom Adams. They're all dead now. Three of 'em died here in Parmele, one every six months. All the folks are dead."

Blanche, who worked 35 years as Parmele's postmaster before her retirement in 1970, lives alone in the big house now. All her children and grandchildren are in other places. As she sits on the front porch reminiscing, a switching engine can be heard at work nearby, out of sight.

"Oh, Lord," she says, "there's been so much changes. If I could just put it all in words."

The Highway Promoter

ROBERSONVILLE   At Williamston, U.S. 64 not only picks up U.S. 13 for a 20-mile stretch to Bethel, it also picks up a name: R.B. Nelson Highway.

Thirteen miles westward, after the highway has become Academy Street on its passage through Robersonville, a state-erected sign identifies an old two-story yellow house at the corner of Broad Street as the home of R.B. Nelson himself. It is the only such sign in front of a private home in the state.

So who is R.B. Nelson and why does he rate such treatment?

Well, he is North Carolina's only officially designated highway promoter. Indeed, America's only.

Just what does a highway promoter do?

In a pine-panelled sitting room, adorned with family portraits, R.B., whose given names are Robert Burton, unfolds a N.C. highway map and begins rattling off highway numbers, what they used to be, what they are now. There is hardly an area on the entire map that R.B. can't point to and say, "That's some of my work," one of his favorite expressions.

"That 159 that goes to the zoo up at Asheboro, that's some of my work, too," he says. "I put 42 all the way from Asheboro to Colerain in Bertie County; 421, I took it out of downtown Greensboro. I ran 6 right down Patterson Avenue.

"I've changed a whole lot of numbers. I've been changing highways a long time.

Changing highways, that's what a highway promoter does. He looks for highways that could be better served by a different route or a different number, then goes about convincing everybody involved that they should be changed.

It is work to which R.B., a short, roly-poly man with curly white hair, has devoted 37 of his 78 years, work that is difficult and frustrating, work that has demanded untold hours for which he has never been paid, work on which he has spent a small fortune of his own money and sacrificed numerous cars.

So why does he do it?

"Everybody have a hobby, don't they?" asks R.B., who speaks with an impediment. "Some like fishing, some hunting. Some play golf, some the horses. I like highways."

Maybe this strange affection for highways goes back to his youth, when as a teenager he helped build the highway that now passes by his front door, then state route 90, later to become U.S. 64. It

58

R.B. Nelson

did not manifest itself until years later.

R.B., son of a doctor, went away to N.C. State College and studied electrical engineering, but the only time he worked in that field was during World War II in Jacksonville, Fla. It was on trips back home to see his family that he really got to thinking about highways. He had to travel on roads with a lot of different numbers and it struck him that it would be easier if he could follow a single number.

"People going from one place to the next, they get confused," he says. "If they have one number they can follow, they can keep that in their head and remember the route. If you had to go on six or eight different roads, you'd get awfully confused."

When R.B. moved back home after the war, he began studying highway maps, and in 1947, the year that his parents died and left him four farms and several rental properties, he decided that what eastern North Carolina needed was a new U.S. Highway. And he knew just the one: U.S. 13.

That highway had begun in Delaware as a spur between the DuPont plant and the city of Wilmington, then had been extended the length of the state, across a chunk of Maryland and down the eastern shore of Virginia to the point where the ferry crossed the Chesapeake Bay to Norfolk.

R.B. wanted to extend the highway from Norfolk to Charleston, S.C. So he picked a route, which involved changing the numbers of several existing highways, and went to work trying to convince everybody along the route and the state highway department that it was the thing to do. He went to every chamber of commerce along the way, to meeting after meeting of county, city and town boards, to offices and meetings in Raleigh and Washington.

"See, it takes a lot of time working on this stuff," he says. "You can't go at it all at one time. You have a lot of argument. Oh, hell yes. Fight like hell, every damn thing.

"You just got to keep meeting with people, keep talking to 'em, get 'em to change. That's the only way you can get it, by work. I've been to many cities, been turned down, go right back again. I don't give up. I'm too determined. I'm determined to see who I want to see. Let me tell you something, only way you get anywhere is to keep right on fighting. I keep fighting till I get what I want."

By 1961, he had what he wanted, although he'd had to alter his route and cut out Charleston. U.S. 13 had been extended from Norfolk to a point just north of Fayetteville, where it now deadends into I-95. It ran right by R.B.'s house, and when the highway signs were being put up, R.B.'s wife, Mae Dell, who died in 1978, asked the state to put one in front of the house so R.B. could see it from his bedroom window.

By then, R.B. had wider dreams for the highway. He wanted it to stretch from Montreal to New Orleans and he set about trying to make it happen. He has since given up hope of extending it beyond its northern terminus at Princeton, N.J., but he has continued working to get it to New Orleans and believes he will succeed.

"As soon as they build a bridge on 401 up there by Fayetteville," he says, "when they build that bridge, then I'll have it all the way to Athens, Ga."

As soon as he got the highway from Norfolk to Fayetteville, R.B. also started another crusade. He wanted the highway named for him, and he began going back to all the chambers of commerce, all the city, town and county boards seeking their endorsements. It took him 14 years, but in 1975, U.S. 13 in North Carolina became the R.B. Nelson Highway, and Gov. James Holshouser appointed R.B. as the state's only highway promoter.

"I'm a highway promoter for life," he says. "Don't make no difference who comes in up there at Raleigh, who goes out. They can't put me out. I proved why I won my role."

It is a role that he takes very seriously, and one that he has expanded to many other roads, often at the request of local or state officials, driving an average of 40,000 miles a year, all at his own expense, always without pay.

"I've worked in 13 states and two provinces of Canada changing highways," he says. "I reckon I'm going to do it till they put me in the hole. It's something I like. It's my hobby. It's a great hobby, too. I'm working on a gang of 'em right now."

Using a cane, he goes into the next room and returns carrying an armful of large papers, rolled and tied with rubber bands—plans for new highways.

"Here's one I'm working on," he says, unrolling one of the papers. "This is going to be 92. See, I'm going to tie in down here in Beaufort County, take it down here, along here, up here . . . ."

Three Rooms, No Bath

BETHEL   It's an old sharecropper shanty on the side of the highway, squeezed between cultivated fields, now devoid of crops.

A shotgun house, it is called, three little rooms in a row, perched on slanty brick pillars. A tipsy brick chimney rises from the middle room, a few bricks missing at top. A flimsy tin-roofed porch droops at the front. The outside walls are covered with a patchwork of tarpaperlike siding designed to look like bricks, colored a dingy yellowish-beige.

No sharecropper lives here, hardly any cropper at all, but there is a small garden in the back where Eula Mae Williams is hoeing. She is a short, squat woman of indeterminate age who doesn't know how old she is. Neither does she know how long she's been living in this house with her mother, Beulah, and sister, Mary.

"Only way I come over here, a dog bit me," she says. "Dog bit me, I started stayin' here then. Had to go to the doctor, took stitches in my laig. My sister, she had two strokes. She and my mama stayed here first. We been livin' here a long time. See, the bossman died. He's dead now, been dead. He own this house. Now Miz Reba own it. We pays rent."

The rent is only $25 a month, but the accommodations are less than desirable. Windows are sealed shut and screenless. Doors, too, are without screens. It is stifling inside on a hot summer day. "Sometimes can't hardly stand it at night," Eula Mae says.

There are no closets inside. Clothes hang on unpainted plywood walls. The tiny kitchen is without running water.

The outhouse stands in weeds behind the house at woods edge. It is covered with old roofing metal, its door ajar.

"I don't go out there," Eula Mae says. "Lot of snakes out there. Go out in the woods sometimes, I git me a bucket in the house at night, use that. Never had a bathroom in our life."

At the back of the house is a rusty hand pump that provides water but demands diligent effort. Eula Mae primes it with murky water from a dirty plastic cup.

"You got to keep on, keep on pumpin'," she says, just before water, clear and cool, begins to flow.

Beside the pump lies a plastic bag, partially filled with aluminum cans picked from the roadside.

"My mama, she pick 'em up, sell 'em to peoples," Eula Mae explains.

Her mama has been peeking from the back door, where dish

Eula Mae Williams

water is puddled next to the concrete block steps. She is a short woman, broad-shouldered and stooped, with a weathered face, her thin, graying hair knotted into plaits. She has no idea of her age.

"I don't know how ol' my mama is," Eula Mae says. "She purty ol' 'ough. My mama, she had a lot of chil'ren."

The day before, her mother had picked cucumbers for a short time on a nearby farm, but she can't work the way she used to.

"Come to gittin' hot, I set down and rest," she says with a big grin, exposing only a few stumps of teeth.

"She'll git out, kinda work," Eula Mae says, "but my mama used to work, used to break ground."

"I used to work," Beulah repeats, grinning. "Used to swall on a ditch bank. Swall with a briar knife. Cut dem weeds down."

"I ain't never had a job," Eula Mae says, and goes on to relate a list of past ailments, of long stays at hospitals. "I'd like to git me a job, 'ough. Little house cleanin' for white peoples, somethin' like 'at. I gits a welfare check. My mama git a check, my sister git one and I git one. We pay bills, light bills, rent."

It is two miles to town, and there is no transportation, no telephone. "Had a telephone," Eula Mae says, "but different peoples come, make calls way off, Washington, D.C., and places like 'at. The man took it back."

A cousin takes them places they have to go. The same cousin comes each morning to tend to Mary's special needs and cook food to leave for the rest of the day. This day she has left fried bream, corn bread and Kool-Aid for supper. Fish is one of Beulah's favorite foods. "Fish and pork chops, chicken noodle soup."

The thing that most occupies the attentions of Beulah, Eula Mae and Mary is the small black and white television in the front room. It plays day and night. There is no argument about their favorite shows.

"George Jefferson and Andy Griffith," Eula Mae says. "Lord, I like 'at. My mama like 'at, don't you Beulah?"

Beulah grins and nods agreement.

"If you could have anything you want," Eula Mae is asked, "what would it be?"

"I would like to have me a nice decent house, really. Where I could have me a bathroom and some water. We need a house bad. This house ain't no good. We tell 'em folks to fix this house. They won't do it."

"See, ol' porch is broke down, look here," Beulah says. "Come out here and break your laig or somethin'."

"That hole," Eula Mae says pointing to the broken porch. "What if my mama fall in that hole in that porch? We really need a house. Welfare said they was goin' to git us a house, but they ain't. We need one bad. I would like to live in one of them private houses like they have in town. Have me a bathroom. We have to go out the door. I git ashamed to go out the door."

A Monument to Blacks

PRINCEVILLE   "This is the oldest incorporated black community in the United States," says the mayor, Jesse Baker, leaning back in his chair. "It actually dates back before the Civil War. It was the first place in this area where the Emancipation Proclamation was read. It was on that hill right by the stoplight, Princeville's one and only stoplight."

Freedom Hill, the community called itself then. It had been settled by a small group of free blacks on the south bank of the Tar River across from the colonial town of Tarboro at a point that would later become the intersection of U.S. highways 64 and 258. After the Civil War, more freed blacks flocked to the settlement. When the town was incorporated in 1885, the name was changed to Princeville, in honor of a prominent local resident, Turner Prince.

It was always a poor town, its narrow streets rutted and muddy, its houses mostly shanties, its people a cheap source of labor for Tarboro and nearby farms.

"All my life, the people in Princeville depended on farmers," recalls W. Ray Matthewson, who is 69 and was for 20 years mayor of the town. "We chopped cotton, plowed, did tobacco work, picked cotton. That was all the work we could get, day work. We didn't have no trades. The farmers would come and carry us out in wagons, later trucks, pay 75 cents a day."

Not everybody in Princeville depended on field labor or domestic jobs in the elegant houses of Tarboro for their livings. There were bootleggers in Princeville and party houses where women entertained men, often white men from across the river. All too frequently there was violence, too.

Many people found themselves without hope and left the town. "They went north, that's where they went," says another former mayor, Ed Bridgers, who's 64. "They went to Baltimore and Washington and Detroit and sent their children back home for their grandparents to raise."

"Most of our friends, they left and went north looking for better times," says Ray Matthewson, who did the same thing himself. "I left and went to Philadelphia for a while. I just wanted to try it. I thought I could make more than 75 cents a day. I went during the Depression, stayed nearly a year. I couldn't stand those soup lines. Had to beg jobs."

That wasn't the only reason he came back home, though.

"Well," he says, "I had a love of Princeville, You had to love the

65

place to ever want to live here. It was flooded two or three times a year, especially in the spring. People who lived on the low ground would have to move."

Floods were the plague of Princeville and almost its undoing.

Devastating floods struck the town two years after its founding, again in 1919, 1924, 1940 and 1958. The worst was in 1919 when the waters swept a drowned mule into one house and left it lying on a bed.

After each flood more people moved away from the town, and in 1958, when the fourth highest flood in the town's history came, Ray Matthewson, then the mayor, decided something had to be done.

"Everybody that ever meant anything to Princeville left," he says, "all but the Matthewsons and Bridgers. We met in the school yard."

After the 1940 flood, Ray's brother, Glennie, who owned the major store in town and was mayor until his death in 1954, had conceived the idea of a dam along the town's edge to protect it from the river.

"We'd read about dikes in Holland, but we didn't know anything about that," Ray says. "We just called it a dam. My brother thought of it, but we didn't have any way to get anybody to do anything."

This time Ray took the idea to the state, and a proposal was drawn and approved for the Army Corps of Engineers to build a 2.5-mile dike along the river at a cost of about $4 million. But first the town had to acquire the right-of-way. Town residents who owned property on the river gave most of the right-of-way, but some non-residents who owned rental property there wanted money.

That was something Princeville didn't have. Its tax base was very small, and the taxes it did collect, only a few hundred dollars a year, were paid voluntarily.

So Ray turned to the Edgecombe County commissioners for help.

"That was the greatest fight I ever had," he recalls.

The town needed only $25,000, but he and Ed Bridgers, a member of the town board, had to go to every commission meeting for several years to plead for the dike. They got it only after they worked out a deal in which the town assigned to the county for 10 years the $1,000 a year it got in revenue sharing for the sale of alcoholic beverages.

The dike was completed in 1967, and it was Ray Matthewson's proudest accomplishment.

"That was the savior for Princeville," he says.

It also was a new beginning for the town.

Ed Bridgers, who followed Ray into office, got a water system for the town in 1976. A year later, he got a sewage system, and Princeville's outhouses went the way of the rusty hand water pumps.

Princeville still has no downtown business section, no factories or places of large employment (most residents work in Tarboro, or in the large plants that have moved into the county in recent years). It still doesn't even have a post office, although it is a town of some

2,300 people. It also still is about 90 per cent black (whites have lived in Princeville for as long as anybody in the town can remember. A family of whites, the Mewborns, operated a grist mill on the river from early in this century, and members of the family still live on the site. Two whites served on the town board in the '70s, but it is currently all black.) Yet a visitor who hadn't seen the town in 15 years might not recognize the place today.

The narrow, rutted streets have been paved and many have sidewalks. Zoning brought the demolition of the worst shanties, and in their place are modern new federally subsidized apartment projects. There is even a park.

Jesse Baker can be credited with these accomplishments. He was appointed mayor four years ago, after another mayor had run up a huge deficit.

"We almost lost the town charter," he says.

He raised taxes and instituted austerity measures, and the town is just now pulling back into the black.

Jesse is 36 years old, a man of great girth and intelligence, a lawyer who also holds an embalming license. Like Ray and Ed, he grew up in Princeville and also moved away for a while as a young man, but he went away to New York to law school.

"I'm a child of the '60s," he says. "I went to law school, quote, to help my people, end quotes. I never intended to do anything but come back."

Jesse, who plans not to seek reappointment as mayor when his term ends in December, 1985, thinks he has been able to help his people and he feels good about it.

"I liked being able to get some of these old people out of these shacks and into decent housing," he says.

Ed Bridgers, still a member of the town board, also feels good about his part in helping Princeville. As a young man, he went off to work in the shipyards at Newport News, but after fighting both in Europe and the Pacific in World War II, he returned home, became a barber and eventually took over his father's small store, which he has turned into a modern convenience store.

"I'm glad I stayed," he says. "Princeville has been good to me. I made a normal living here and saw some of the things I desired to see that was impossible back when I was a boy."

"The way I was trying to make Princeville," says Ray Matthewson, who is retired now, "I just wanted to better the situation, because I live here, my people are here. I hadn't even thought about integration or anything. All we wanted was to make a living, not be in any racket like bootlegging, being up in court, chain gangs, stuff like that. We wanted to better our conditions and live here. We believe like Booker T. Washington said. Cast your buckets down where you are. Make a success of where you live."

In a brief history that Mary Matthewson, former principal of Princeville School and widow of Glennie Matthewson, wrote about the town before her death is this paragraph: "Princeville may be no monument in terms of steel, bricks and concrete, but in terms of what it has produced against constrictive odds, it's about as fine a monument as Blacks have anywhere. Princeville is, and has been, 'the Black Experience' in America. Like the Black man, Princeville has endured and has assured itself of a future second to none."

The Oldest Town

TARBORO   Near Princeville, the highway divides. The bypass swings south of Princeville and around the southern and western edges of Tarboro. The old highway, 64 business, proceeds through Princeville, crosses the Tar River and becomes Tarboro's Main Street.

As with most towns where bypasses have been built, the town of Tarboro has moved out to meet the new road. The major motel, the mall, the new high school, the city park, gas stations, car dealers, fast-food joints, the town's only fancy steak house, the big headquarters of Carolina Telephone with its acres of meticulously tended employee vegetable gardens by the road—all line the bypass.

In most towns that have been bypassed and malled, the downtown business district is dead or dying, but Tarboro offers a surprise. To cross the river bridge onto Main Street is to cross into another era. Downtown Tarboro not only thrives, it shines.

The facades of almost every downtown building have been restored to original condition. Garish signs have been removed and colorful awnings overhang new brick sidewalks decorated with young oaks and replicas of the town's original electric street lamps.

Anchoring the south end of Main Street, near the river, is a new $14 million retirement center, the Albemarle, and on the north is the town common, where monuments are sheltered by huge oaks. The common was set aside when the town was founded in 1760, one of only a few town commons in all the South.

Tarboro is not only the oldest town on U.S. 64, but perhaps the most revitalized, and recently it has been getting a lot of attention.

USA Today, the national newspaper, featured Tarboro in a front-page article headlined "Rebirth of Main Street U.S.A.," and Southern Living Magazine also carried a big spread on the town. Other towns send committees to study Tarboro.

"Tarboro is a beautiful, almost perfect small town," says Watson Brown, the town's director of planning and economic development. "It's got the beauty, the quality of life, and what we're doing, we're using our history, the beauty of the town and the quality of life to draw investors to the town. Everything you see here you can put quality in front of it. We don't want growth at any cost."

Wat, as most people in town call him, is 33. He was born in Tarboro, a town of 10,600 people that found early prosperity in

69

cotton. He grew up six miles south of town. "All my family lives here and has for 150 years," he says.

Wat grew up with a love of the area's heritage, especially for its grand old houses, and he studied historic preservation while getting his master's degree in urban design at the University of North Carolina at Chapel Hill. He was in Savannah applying for a job in 1974 when his mother called to tell him that Tarboro had decided to hire its first planner. He came home to apply that afternoon and has since been at the core of Tarboro's revitalization.

That revitalization actually began in 1963 when several prominent townspeople got so upset over the destruction of the old town hall that they formed a historic preservation society, but it wasn't until the mid-'70s that things really got moving.

Since the effort began, some $20 million has been invested; the downtown business district has been restored; the Pender Museum, featuring historical items from the area, has been opened in an old house; an old cotton press has been restored and moved to the town common; a kudzu-covered gulch has been transformed into a nature trail; the Blount-Bridgers house, an 1808 federal mansion built by Thomas Blount, one of the founders of Raleigh, has been turned into a cultural center including a gallery displaying the works of famous American painter Hobson Pittman, who was born and reared in Tarboro; a drive has begun to save the town's dozens of historic homes, some of them nearly 200 years old; and the U.S. Department of the Interior has established a National Recreation trail through the town's 45-block historic district.

One result is that Tarboro has found itself the object of tourists' attentions. Nobody plans a vacation in Tarboro, but it has become a prime trip-break stop for people on their way to other places, and tourism has increased 65 percent in the last two years, which means that word is getting out about the town. Some residents still talk about the fellow from Germany who showed up a while back saying he'd heard about Tarboro while visiting California.

"We're not going to be like Williamsburg and we don't want to be," Wat says. "God knows, that would be terrible. We're just starting. We're a nice stopover place, and what we're hoping is that people will come here and get so turned on by the town they decide they want to invest here."

More and more of that is happening. Visitors have opened shops on Main Street. People from as far away as Florida, California and Boston have bought, or expressed an interest in buying, old houses to restore and move into.

So successful and enthusiastic has been Tarboro's preservation effort that it has spread to the county. Louise Boney, a 24-year-old Duke University graduate from Greensboro who works with Wat Brown, was hired last year to save some 100 endangered old mansions in Edgecombe County, and she is seeking buyers nationally.

Wat is unconcerned that an influx of outsiders might change the character of the place he loves, on which he has spent so much effort to preserve and renew.

"We're getting some good new people moving in, which is good for the town, but I don't see Tarboro becoming a town that focuses on out-of-towners. Tarboro still has a lot of homes lived in by some of the same families that built them and lived in them for generations. And more and more of the young current generation are staying here or moving back. They're seeing that Tarboro has a lot to offer."

House of Regret

TARBORO   She hardly can bear to look at the house anymore, but she hardly can stop talking about it. It's never very far from her thoughts.

"This house is in ruins now," she says, offering a brochure about it prepared by the Historic Preservation Fund of North Carolina. "My house. I sold it to a fellow I thought was going to restore it and he didn't. It's falling down."

The Farrar-Martin House, it is called on the brochure, although it was always known around town as just the Farrar House. It is a two-story, L-shaped house fast by Trade Street near downtown with ornate trimming and massive chimneys arising from its slate roof. Its interior boasts a curving staircase and marble fireplaces in every downstairs room. The house was built about 1875 by O.C. Farrar, one of Tarboro's most prominent men of the time. He owned a cotton mill, a hotel on Main Street, a general store. He was grandfather of Mary Marshall Farrar Martin, but she never knew him.

"My grandfather helped get this town started after the war," she says. "During Reconstruction, he got this town going. He had a seat on the cotton exchange in New York. He built the Baptist church down here. He came here from Granville County, and he died at 50 from dysentery.

"He built this house. My father was born in this house. My grandmother moved there as a bride in 1876. I had tears, I had happiness and fun in this house. I grew up there. My children grew up there. I feel so bad that it's falling down."

Mary Marshall is a perfect guide for a tour of Tarboro, a historic town that missed by only two votes becoming state capital 200 years ago. Not only are Mary Marshall's roots deep in the town, but she involves herself in things, and she seems to know everybody in town—who lives in every house and the story behind it.

"I used to know everything that was walking around up here and so did everybody else," she says, as she steers her Ford LTD down a side street, "but I don't anymore."

A tour with Mary Marshall is not only a look into Tarboro's past but a glimpse into her own. It begins on Trade Street.

"That was my house," she says of the deteriorating old house, locked and empty. "That's where I lived. It just makes me sick."

The house sits across the street from the Dozier House, an 1859 house restored by the town for offices, which soon will also house the Chamber of Commerce. It is catercornered from the oldest house

72

Mary Marshall Farrar Martin at church her grandfather built

in town, a small, green-shuttered white frame house on Church Street, built in 1790, that is home for retired teacher Mary Latham.

On Main Street, Mary Marshall points to a corner now occupied by the Eagle Variety Store. "That was the Farrar Hotel," she says, "and I was born there, upstairs. It was three stories high, and my daddy ran it. Ripley put it in his column that it was advertised as the worst hotel in the state."

Her father died in 1943, and the hotel was torn down in 1965.

It was her father's death that brought Mary Marshall back to Tarboro the one time she left.

"When I was young I wanted to go to a city and catch the world by the tail," she says at lunch in a new downtown restaurant that features a quiche of the day.

She chose Richmond, where she got a job at Thalhimers. She was working there when she met the man who would be her husband, Prescott L. Martin, a native of Spartanburg, a Citadel graduate who had become a dashing officer in the Army Air Corps. After her father's death, Mary Marshall returned to Tarboro to stay with her mother, and Prescott came to court and marry her and settle into the house her grandfather built. It was there that they made their lives and reared their three children.

But after the children were grown and gone, the big house seemed empty. They didn't need all that space. The upkeep was getting more and more costly, the heating bills preposterous. So they decided to put the house up for sale to somebody who would restore it. In 1979, they sold it and moved into a spacious apartment in an 1858 mansion, the Barracks, so named because it was thought to have been built on the site of a Revolutionary War encampment. The buyer, a fellow from upstate who had big plans that never materialized, lost the house and it later was sold to an architect from California, who so far has left it to deteriorate and to cause Mary Marshall daily grief and regret.

"It is just a shame what has happened to that house," she says, as she resumes her tour. "I wouldn't have sold it if I'd known what was going to happen."

She is disappointed that the town character, a bicycle-riding fellow who daily adorns his body with Jesse Helms paraphernalia and preaches the glories of his hero on a Main Street corner, is not at his accustomed post, so she takes a turn by his house, where half a dozen U.S. and N.C. flags line the sidewalk, which is overhung by a huge British flag near the porch.

The tour includes such Tarboro highlights as the recently restored Blount-Bridgers House, the town cultural center, with its gallery of paintings by Tarboro native Hobson Pittman, whose works hang in America's most prestigious museums, and Calvary Episcopal Church, designed by architect William Percival and built before the Civil War, with its signed Tiffany windows and its churchyard of nearly 100 varieties of exotic trees, most of them nearly a century and a half old—one of the finest such collections in the country.

But the tour also takes in such lesser known spots as the downtown lot where David Pender started a little grocery which grew into the D.P. Stores, which became Colonial Stores, which became Big Star Supermarkets; the spot where George Allen Holderness started a one-operator telephone company which grew into Carolina Telephone, which now serves most of eastern North Carolina; and the little warehouse by the river where F.S. Royster started a guano company in 1885.

F.S. Royster, a first cousin of Mary Marshall's grandfather, came to Tarboro to work in his cousin's general store.

74

"This is a story that was told to me," says Mary Marshall, "I don't know whether it's true, but he was supposed to have gone to my grandfather and told him he wanted to go into business and asked him to go in with him, but my grandfather was having a bad year and couldn't spare the money, and look what happened."

What happened was that around the turn of the century Royster moved his fertilizer company to Norfolk where it became a huge corporation.

In east Tarboro, the black section, Mary Marshall stops her car in front of a white frame church.

"This was First Baptist Church," she says. "My grandfather gave this church. He gave the land, helped build it. He died right before it was finished. His funeral was the first ever held in that church. It's just like it was. The organ, everything is still in there. It's darling on the inside. I wish we could see it."

The church was moved from Main Street in 1929 and a new, more imposing brick church was built in its place. It is now St. Paul's Baptist. After trying the doors and finding them locked, Mary Marshall calls at a house across the street, and soon Florence Arnold, a member of the church for 50 years, comes from her home with a key. The two are old acquaintances, and the talk is of children and past events.

"Oh, y'all've changed the pews," is the first thing Mary Marshall says when she steps inside the church.

Not only are the pews new, but so are the shiny chandeliers.

"I wish y'all hadn't changed it," says Mary Marshall, her voice heavy with disappointment. "Last time I came in here it was just like it was. What y'all got rid of is what people want nowadays. They want old things."

Old houses is one thing Tarboro is blessed with, and Mary Marshall points out the special ones as she resumes her tour. This yellow one, which is for sale, was the home of the father of movie actor Joseph Cotten. This one was built by F.S. Royster. The young couple who bought that big one on the corner have been painting it for three years.

"This house right here," she says, pointing out another two-story Victorian, "was copied after the one I lived in, but mine is better. The Archives of History says mine is the best Victorian of the era. It was beautiful when I lived there. It just makes me sick every time I think about what's happened to that house."

The Millionaire Yard Boy

TARBORO   He is master of the house now, but it was different when he first came to it 51 years ago. He was 15 then.

"I used to be the yard boy," Joe Grayiel says. "Kept the yard clean, cut the grass, things like that."

The couple who lived in the house, Aubrey and Maud Leggett, were childless. Aubrey owned a plantation in a nearby community that bears his family name. Maud was the only child of John Shackelford, who started Riverview Knitting Mills, said by folks in Tarboro to be the first knitting mill in the South. She had been born in this big house on Main Street in 1888, had inherited it at her father's death two years before she married Aubrey in 1922.

After Joe started working for the Leggetts, they took such a liking to him that they went to his parents, who had two other sons, and asked if Joe could come live with them and be full-time handyman. Joe liked the Leggetts, liked the work, and his father, a blacksmith, gave permission.

Joe moved into the house in 1933, and he has never left it.

After Aubrey's death in 1940, Joe, who never married, became almost indispensable to Maud, who became more reclusive as years passed.

"I was the cook, the maid, kept everything repaired, tended to business, farmed," says Joe. "Wasn't nothin' I didn't do."

Miss Maud, as she was known in the town, died in November 1979, and when her will was filed, Joe assumed a new significance in Tarboro.

"Her estate was five million dollars," says Joe, "and she left it all to me. She *left* it to me. I didn't get it all. The government got 48 per cent, the state got 12 per cent, and the bank got 5 per cent. That's where an estate goes to. They get 65 per cent and they don't want no land, no house, nothin' like that. They want cash and they want it now."

Although he didn't like it, paying wasn't that great a strain for Joe.

"Well, I had enough in the estate to take care of it. I had to sell right much of my stocks and some bonds."

He managed to retain the plantation, some downtown properties and, most importantly, the house.

It is an unusual house, a three-story Victorian on half a downtown block, hidden behind a high brick wall, the only house in the business district of Main Street, which Joe maintains should be St. George Street, which it was when the town was founded in 1760. The house

Joe Grayiel (left) with twin brother George

was built of brick, then covered with stucco designed to look like large gray stone blocks. Corner blocks are painted subdued red, and the gingerbread trim is red and yellow.

Now in the National Register of Historic Places, the house has 14 rooms, four baths and a separate kitchen out back. Dormer windows peek from the slate roof. A 150-year-old magnolia graces the front yard, a fenced formal garden the back.

"It's a comfortable old house," says Joe, "and it's a nice old house."

Joe lives in it with his twin brother, George, who retired after 39 years with the post office, the two of them sharing a single bedroom. Joe has made one concession to his new wealth and position. He no longer cooks except on special occasions. The brothers, who are a familiar sight on downtown streets, dressed daily in identical suits and ties, take lunch every day at a senior citizens center, dinner each night at different restaurants.

Joe, who daily wears a flower in his lapel, is a history buff who delights in telling local history and showing occasional invited visitors the historic items in his own historic house.

"Everything in the house has been with the house and came with

77

the house," he says. "Nothing in the house came from an antique store or has been reproduced."

Downstairs rooms have frescoed walls, some with gilded trim, and inlaid wooden floors, a different pattern in every room. Fireplaces are Italian marble, chandeliers silver.

"This is the parlor," says Joe, entering a downstairs front room where Miss Maud, a graduate of the University of Virginia and the Conservatory of Music in Boston, once entertained visitors on a grand piano.

"When she played, she played with style," Joe says, plunking unstylishly on the recently tuned keys.

Portraits of Miss Maud's parents adorn one wall and a portrait of her graces another. Joe bristles at some townspeoples' depiction of his benefactor as a reclusive eccentric who grew feebleminded in her later years.

"She was a typical Southern lady in every respect. She had the manners, the quietness and the dignity of a typical Southern lady. She was refined in her actions in every way. She was an outgoing person. She believed in taking care of animals (Joe still has two of her cats and her beloved 13-year old Chihuahua, Cindy) and taking care of things of history and taking care of business. Two weeks before she died, she bought a hundred thousand dollars worth of North Carolina bonds. That's how healthy she was, and she knew what those bonds were paying, too."

In the library, Joe displays Indian artifacts from the area: Civil War memorabilia (including a lock of Jefferson Davis's baby hair), a snuff box supposedly owned by Marie Antoinette, and rare books.

One book he keeps in a special place is priceless. It is a hymnal, handwritten in 1739 by John Wesley, founder of the Methodist Church, who made seven of the leather-bound books for his students. Only two are known to exist, and the other is incomplete.

In 1981, the book and a large amount of silver were stolen from the house in a break-in, and international police agencies and rare book dealers around the world were alerted. The book was recovered four months later after an anonymous tipster called officers and said it could be found in an abandoned farmhouse near Rocky Mount.

Joe kept the book in a safe deposit box only briefly before returning it to the house, which since has been so thoroughly wired with burglar alarms that merely passing from room to room requires shutting down parts of the system.

"If you keep it in a safe deposit box," he says, "You can't show it to anybody."

Other rooms contain silver once owned by the Vanderbilts and displays of Miss Maud's huge collection of rare glassware. On the second floor, Joe opens a musty, hidden-away closet to reveal another large collection of glassware—this a clutter of dusty, filled bottles.

"This is my booze closet. I guess some of that mess came out of the old house," he says, referring to the 18th century frame home of Miss Maud's grandfather that once stood on the site. "Ain't no tellin' what's in there. Somebody asked me, 'Why don't you pour that mess down the sink?' I said, 'I may decide to start drinking.'"

Steep narrow steps lead to the attic.

"Come on, I'll take you up to yesteryear," Joe says. "I keep the ghosts and spooks up here."

It is a perfect spot indeed for ghosts of the past, for in this spacious stuffy room are Miss Maud's childhood toys, her doll houses and baby carriage and dozens of other old family heirlooms, including a loaded pistol her husband's father carried through the Civil War and the family's first radio, one of the first made.

"I don't know why they built this room, unless it was just to keep stuff like this," Joe says. "You know, I feel sorry for people who live in trailers because they don't have room to store anything."

Outside, Joe shows off the old kitchen with its huge wood stove on which he has cooked many meals, the only cook stove in the house.

"I'm going to paint the kitchen next week," he says.

Tall ladders lean against the back of the house, where Joe has been painting in recent days, a constant chore since he came to the house at 15. When it is suggested to him that one of the benefits of inheriting wealth might be having to paint no more, Joe only laughs.

"If I hired the painting out, what'd I be doin'? If I was about 35, I can tell you what I'd be doin', but 66 put a stop to that."

What about travel? He could take a cruise. A woman he has been dating, a teacher, is doing just that, seeing Alaska. On this very day he has received from her a having-a-great-time postcard. Joe snorts at the notion.

"She tells me how wonderful Alaska is. Well, who's better off, me sittin' here enjoying myself, or her off up there pushin' herself? I love Tarboro. I'm content right here. If you can find a better place, I don't know where it'd be.

"You know, the town wondered what would happen to me after they found out about the will, if I was going to change and become a big shot, a big spender."

He grins.

"They found out it didn't change me at all. I'm still the good fellow I always was.

"I'd give anything to live my life over again. I don't know a lot of changes I'd make. I'd liked to have learned to played a musical instrument. Maybe I ought to have gotten married and had some children. That's the only two things I might change."

Passage

West of Tarboro, the contour of the land changes. There are gentle dips and rises now, and even the soil itself is different, not so rich and effluvial, showing in spots an orangish tinge of what is to come.

Behind is the coastal plain with its monotonous and seemingly endless flatness, ahead the Piedmont plateau.

In its first 125 miles, from Whalebone at oceanside to Tarboro on the Tar River, U.S. 64 has climbed only 58 feet, so gradually as to be unnoticeable. In the 15 miles from Tarboro to Rocky Mount, it rises another 40 feet. By the time it reaches Raleigh, just 52 miles beyond Rocky Mount, it will have ascended to 363 feet.

With the change in the land comes change in use. Tobacco is more noticeable, and now among the fields of corn and soybeans are cattle farms, stretches of sweet potato fields, even a few patches of cotton, a reminder of why these fields were first cleared and tilled.

At Heartsease, halfway between Tarboro and Rocky Mount, an old farm has been turned into a trailer park, and farther along, at a fancy, new house, is a fenced field of geese.

As the highway approaches Rocky Mount, the roadside becomes more cluttered: a Free Will Baptist in a small white trailer, houses, junkyards, car lots, fruit stands, the weedy fairgrounds, the broken skeleton of a long dead drive-in theater.

Just east of the city limits, the highway divides again. The old road, 64 business, swings south past the Tower Drive In, a survivor ("Multi Features Nightly, For Adults, Rated X"), into downtown Rocky Mount, a bustling, fast-growing town of 47,000 people, once an agricultural center, now with a healthy industrial mix. The town straddles the mainline tracks of the Seaboard Railroad, which run down the middle of Main Street and form the line separating Nash and Edgecombe counties.

It was on the Edgecombe side of Main Street that North Carolina's first woman pharmacist, Emily Kyser, opened a drugstore with her husband Paul early in this century. They reared a son, Kay, who became a famous bandleader. Not far from where the highway crosses Main Street once stood a ballpark where in 1909 Jim Thorpe, later to become an Olympic gold medal winner in the decathalon, made his professional baseball debut with the Rocky Mount Railroaders.

But most traffic avoids downtown Rocky Mount by swinging onto the new bypass east of town. Here the highway assumes a whole new character, four lanes, divided, built to interstate standards, designed to move traffic quickly. The traveler catches only quick glimpses of Rocky Mount on its northern edge, mostly at overpasses and underpasses: a ball field, apartments, the Tar River, the railroad tracks, the big Hardee's building, the old municipal airport.

On the western side of town, Nash General Hospital looms, a highrise in brown brick, winging in all the directions of the compass, and on the other side of the road the huge plants of London Mills and Texfi. The highway widens dramatically as it approaches Interstate 95, the main road south for Yankee travelers, but the intersection, where 64 passes over 95, is an uncommon one: no gas stations, motels, restaurants, outlet stores, Silly Billy's or Loony Luke's, nothing but trees, grass, shrubs, a stand of kudzu overwhelming a nearby bank.

For the next 35 miles, the highway is a ride through the lushness that is North Carolina, interrupted only by the intrusions of lesser roads passing overhead on concrete spans. The view is of trees (more hardwoods amongst the pines now) and rolling hills, a soybean field here, a tobacco patch there, an old farm house yonder.

The old highway, 64A, cuts in and out, leading to the bypassed country towns of Nashville and Spring Hope, the community of Momeyer. Near the Middlesex intersection of the old road, the highway crosses the Tar River for the fourth and final time, the river much narrower here than at the first crossing near Tarboro.

For a three-mile stretch, the highway passes through the tip of Franklin County, then into Wake County, 22 miles from Raleigh at a picturesque lake lined with docks, boathouses and beautiful homes set in trees back from the water.

Ten miles east of Raleigh, at Knightdale, a single yellow sign, "Freeway Ends," announces another change in the highway's character. It is still four lanes divided by a grassy median, but farms and homes and businesses line the roadside, growing increasingly more congested as the highway closes in on Raleigh, and there are stoplights and dangerous crossovers. At 8 in the morning, the westbound lanes of this entire stretch swell with bumper-to-bumper traffic carrying people to jobs in Raleigh, the first and only real city along the highway on its passage through the state. At 5 in the afternoon the pattern is reversed. Once the highway passed through the center of Raleigh, but that was years ago, and no sign of its route remains. Until 1983 it swung northward on the beltline in a long loop around the city. Now it turns southward for a 13-mile run on the new Tom Bradshaw Freeway, along with U.S. Highways 70 and 401 and Interstate 40. At the point where 64 enters the freeway, it is only four lanes, but two miles along it grows to six, and five miles more to eight. At some points it is 10 lanes wide, and in a few places a single side of the highway boasts six lanes, the equal of any big-city freeway.

Yet it passes through remarkably open country, the highway mostly tree-lined, offering here and there a view of farm fields nestling next to the city, an indication of the state's essentially rural nature. Only at the Person Street exit does the city skyline rise on the northern horizon, while acres of Winn-Dixie warehouses squat beneath the southern side of the highway. On the city's southwestern edge, the highway exits onto U.S. 1, another freeway, past South Hills Shopping Center, where a smiley face decorates the sign of the Happy Inn motel. Four miles westward, it departs U.S. 1, and becomes once again a two-lane highway, heading for the forested red-dirt hills of Chatham County, climbing ever more dramatically as it goes.

Mobile Home Dreams

HEARTSEASE "I'm going back, way back before I knew anything about it," Isaac Calhoun says. "This came about way back in the 1800s, close to 1850, sometime there. A Mr. Hart owned this property. His name was R.G. Hart. I assume he was the one that figured in it being named. I ain't going to tell you when it got its name because I don't know. I really think the name started from a railroad siding out here."

However it came about, it is a comforting name for a community—Heartsease—a soothing sign on the highway almost halfway between Tarboro and Rocky Mount. In the beginning the community was centered around the big white house that R.G. Hart built and several thousand acres of farm land he accumulated. He was a magistrate, had a courtroom in a building behind his house, kept a store there, too, and had a miniature replica of his house for a smokehouse.

All those buildings were gone by the time Isaac bought the big house in 1941, and most of the huge plantation had long since been broken up and sold.

Isaac, who's 80, was born about 10 miles away, the last of 11 children, and grew up there on his father's 110-acre farm. Like his father, he became a farmer, and after his father died, when the family farm was parceled out to the children, Isaac stayed on, farming his share, eventually buying a couple of other shares from his brothers and sisters, renting other nearby land.

Still, it wasn't enough on which to make a living, so Isaac came to Heartsease and bought the old house and 221 acres around it and began growing cotton, corn, tobacco and peanuts.

"I thought it was a big farm when I bought it," he says, "but in a few years, by God, it was about as small as the one I had."

Farming was changing drastically, going from hand labor to almost total mechanization, and that required huge investment and more and more land to turn a profit. When his only son, Ike, decided to go into farming with him, Isaac, who'd started farming with mules and tenant laborers, bought some complicated new equipment, rented some more land. But a couple of years later, when Ike decided farming wasn't really for him and took a job in a Rocky Mount fiber plant, Isaac made a decision.

"I said, 'What the hell do I want to stay out here and work myself to death for?'" he remembers. "So I done the same thing the little farmer had already done before me. I sold out all my equipment and quit."

If Isaac had decided to stay in farming, Heartsease might have remained a community of only a few families, but because he didn't, it now has more than 600 residents, all but a few of them living in mobile homes on Isaac's farm and working in Tarboro and Rocky Mount.

About the time he quit farming, Isaac started fixing up an old tenant house to rent. It was on the highway not far from his house, beside one of three irrigation lakes he'd strung by the roadside. When a county sanitarian came to approve a septic tank for the house, he and Isaac got to talking and the sanitarian looked across the lake at a pasture beyond and made an observation.

"He said, 'That's the prettiest place I've ever seen for a mobile home park,'" Isaac recalls. "I said, 'What you talking about?' He said, 'A mobile home park. You know, a place where a feller could park his trailer and pay a little rent.' I said, 'Ain't no demand for that, is there?' He said, 'Why, yeah. They coming in here and no place to put 'em.' I decided, well, hell, I ain't farming, I'll put in a few and see how I get along. So I started building and the first winter, when the winter come down, I think we had 10 units."

That was in 1966, and the park has been growing ever since, as fast as Isaac could get money to expand it. When the pasture was full, he moved into a corn field, offering bigger lots. Now there are 135 trailers, and Isaac has governmental approval for more as soon as he can afford to put in streets, water lines and septic tanks. Even that wouldn't meet the demand. He has stacks of applications for lots.

To Isaac that demand signifies change in society. "Times and conditions is what makes changes. Your economy makes the changes come about," he says launching into a long explanation of how farming and economy changes brought the mobile home boom.

"When houses kept getting higher and higher and got so damn high a man couldn't afford to make the payments, they had to look for something else. Those folks who couldn't buy a house could go out here and buy a mobile home, furnished, ready to live in for a whole lot less than they could even think about getting a house. It fitted into the picture perfectly. I'm not trying to put a sales job on you, but there's nowhere you can live for as little money and have as good a living quarters as you can in these trailers."

Still, it was a rare person who came to the park and thought of it as a lifetime home.

"When we first started," says Ike, who came back to work with his father as the park grew, "everybody who came out here said it's just temporary until we can get on our feet. We want a brick home."

At lot 102, a lakeside lot on the highway, the charcoal grill is blazing in front of a beige, rust-trimmed trailer, 70 feet long and 14 feet wide. Inside, Glen Webb, who has just finished a day's work at the same fiber plant in Rocky Mount where Ike once worked, is patting out hamburgers for his family's supper. He and his wife,

Pam, both 26, bought this trailer new 15 months ago and found this lot after trying two other parks.

"It just happened to come available," Glen says. "We were lucky."

For six years, Pam and Glen lived in an apartment, but with two small children, they felt cramped and thought they were throwing money away. So they sold their furniture to get a down payment on the trailer, and although they have to pay $55 a month for their lot, they get a tax break and their utility bills are cheaper.

"We like it," says Glen, who has to drive about 14 miles to work. "We like it a lot. We're satisfied with it, just wish it was a little closer to everything. There's a lot of nice people out here, and I've taught the young'uns fishin', they love that."

"We could use more room," says Pam, who has just arrived home from her job at an employment agency, "but this is like heaven compared to an apartment. I wouldn't mind going to a doublewide."

"This is kind of a stepping stone," Glen adds. "We'd like to have a nice brick home someday. That's the American dream, isn't it?"

Some are having to alter that dream. Some residents have lived years at the park. One of the original 10 residents lived there until his death this summer. And some who have already achieved the dream are giving it up.

"You're getting two types now," Ike says. "You're getting the young just starting out, wanting to get into a house. And you're getting others, the retiring who're wanting to get rid of a house and the upkeep. They're coming here to stay. I know of two right now, just moved in here from New York, retired, and this is where they want to go."

In an office behind a convenience store he opened to serve the park, Isaac looks at his dreams framed on the wall. "This is the blueprints for the old park," he says. "Now I'll show you the one on the new park. This is the new park we got approved. We are built up to here and now we're going on over here. There'll be about 225 units here when we get through. We build as fast as our money will let us. Right now, the demand is here. Things are a lot different than they used to be."

The Man Who Sold His Name

ROCKY MOUNT   The name, spelled out in letters nearly a story high atop the six-story building by the side of the highway, is instantly recognizable, not only in this country but also in many other lands.

Hardee's.

"This is the nerve center," says John Merritt in a third-floor cubicle, "the world headquarters of the chain."

Here the big decisions are made: Will the Huskee become the Big Deluxe. Yes. Will the Big Twin, once the Huskee Jr., disappear forever? Yes. Will the Turkey Club be added to the menu? Yes. Will char-broiling be abandoned? Possibly.

In the worldwide hamburger sweepstakes, Hardee's is running neck-and-neck with Wendy's for third place, both of them chasing hard after Burger King, none of them with any real hope of ever catching McDonald's.

Hardee's has some 2,200 restaurants, with an average of four new ones being opened every week. Compare that with about 2,400 for Wendy's, 3,500 for Burger King, and 8,000, more or less, for McDonald's.

Still, even fourth place in this race pays well, Hardee's had sales of $1.95 billion last year.

And the company would have the world believe that it all began just up Church Street from Hardee's headquarters at a small red and white tile building at the intersection of Falls Road. This was the first restaurant opened by Hardee's Drive-Ins Inc., unlike any other Hardee's today and kept almost in its original condition as a company showpiece.

At the headquarters, where the company honors a single founder, Leonard Rawls, with a portrait in the lobby, John Merritt, vice president of public and government affairs, explains that when he came to the company two years ago he was surprised to find no written history of it. So he put together a chronology, mostly from old company reports. The first item on it is this: "Hardee's began September, 1960, with a restaurant opened by Wilbur Hardee in Greenville, North Carolina."

It isn't surprising that John would spell Wilber's first name wrong. He's never met him, never spoken with him, knows nothing about him. After making several calls, he can't find anybody who knows Wilber's whereabouts or what he's doing. At Hardee's, Wilber Hardee is a forgotten man.

86

Wilber Hardee

"This was the little ol' buildin' with the H's out in front," Wilbeı
says, walking into a building on 14th Street in Greenville abuzz with
workers putting up walls, transforming it into a medical clinic. "Boy,
they're makin' this nice, dog if they ain't.

"See this is where the H's used to be, right out front here. Two
H's held the roof up." He grins. "Every damn time somebody walked
out the front, they'd about hit their head over it. That tile there,
that's the original tile. This wall right here's where all the grills were,
in the back here.

"To start off with, we didn't have nothin' but a hamburger and a
cheeseburger. One sold for 15 cents and the cheeseburger was 20.

French fries, drinks, shakes and apple turnovers. That was it. Best menu I ever had. Since then, it's been trouble.

"I tell you, back then, this was *the* location. Hell, they stood in line here all day buying food."

This building near the campus of East Carolina University was the original Hardee's, but the concept for it was anything but original with Wilber.

He had grown up on farms in Martin and Pitt counties, had quit school to help his brother run country gas stations, had even sung in a hillbilly band before going off to the Navy in World War II. He came home and opened a hole-in-the-wall grill in the little town of Winterville, which he gave up for a larger restaurant near Washington, which he gave up for yet another restaurant in Greenville called the Silo.

He was running the Silo in 1960 when a passing salesman told him about a new place in Greensboro that was doing a bang-up business selling 15-cent hamburgers.

So one morning, Wilber got up early and drove to Greensboro, arriving in time for lunch at the new McDonald's on Summit Avenue, which had opened the previous fall. It was the first McDonald's in North Carolina.

"Now McDonald's was small then," he says. "I was checkin' 'em out. What impressed me was, I set out in front there and saw they took in $168 in one hour at lunch. That was big money then, 1960, on 15-cent hamburgers. That was *big* money."

Wilber took a picture of the building, went back home and got a developer to build a near copy of it and rent it to him. Like McDonald's, the building had red and white tiles and walk-up windows, but instead of arches, it had big red H's. Menu and prices were the same, except that Wilber decided the burgers would be better char-broiled than fried.

"The whole world's a copy cat, ain't it?" he says. "Everything's copy cats."

Copy cat or not, it worked. Wilber couldn't believe his good fortune.

"It went great," he says. "It went so damn great from September third to December 31st, my gross profit was ninety-five hundred bucks and that was big, big money for that time."

Word got out about Wilber's success, and that December an accountant from Rocky Mount, Leonard Rawls, came to see him. He had a young friend, Jim Gardner, whose father had a lot in Rocky Mount that would be a good site for another Hardee's. They could get money to expand. A deal was struck, a corporation formed. Wilber got half of Hardee's, Leonard and Jim the other half. No money, says Wilber, changed hands.

"I didn't get a damn thing. We just joined hands. We were going to branch out."

They opened the second Hardee's on Church Street in Rocky Mount in May 1961. By then plans were already being made to sell franchises and open other stores, and Wilber was dissatisfied. The three partners were all company directors, and under the contract they'd signed decisions were made by a majority vote of the directors, says Wilber. That gave the other two control, so in June Wilber sold out to them.

"I got out because when I realized what the contract was, I saw I didn't have anything," he says. "I sold out for $20,000. Sold my name."

Hardee's grew quickly. By 1963 it had become a public corporation. By 1964 there were 59 Hardee's around the Southeast, some of them with the new unusual pagoda design the company adopted for a few years. Jim Gardner ran unsuccessfully for Congress. The new headquarters building, two stories of it, went up in 1966, the year Gardner got elected to Congress and left the company, and by 1968, when Gardner ran unsuccessfully for governor, there were 151 Hardee's and earnings were looking good. (Gardner went into a motel chain that failed and now has a chain of barbecue restaurants based in Rocky Mount).

In 1972, the company acquired a Midwest hamburger chain called Sandy's, creating 213 new Hardee's, and the following year Leonard Rawls stepped up to chairman of the board while Jack Laughery, former president of Sandy's, became president.

Growth continued through the 1970s, with Hardee's spreading all over this country and around the world, and in 1978 a Canadian conglomerate called Imasco Ltd. bought into the company. Two years later, Imasco, which has interests in tobacco, beauty products, prescription drugs, sporting goods and other products, bought the remainder of Hardee's stock, and Leonard Rawls was replaced as chairman of the board (he died in 1982 after trying to start a chain of Chinese restaurants).

Now the Canadian flag flies alongside those of the United States and North Carolina in front of the big Hardee's headquarters, and on the third floor John Merritt talks about changes and the future.

"Consumers tastes are changing all the time. The menus are changing as America's tastes are changing. You just have to go on. You can't look back in this industry. One thing you can be sure of, if you do not change in this industry, you will absolutely perish. McDonald's is having to change, and they're the least adaptable to change.

"Everybody keeps a close eye on everybody else all the time. They're testing stuff all the time. It's a more sophisticated society and a more sophisticated industry than it used to be. It's changed a heck of a lot since Wilber Hardee got in the business."

"If you want to know the truth about it," Wilber says, "I was stupid, that's what I was. You know how it is, you make mistakes. I won't make many more in my life, I don't reckon. I got some good learnin' out of what I did, though."

He is 65 now, with a bit of a paunch and hair tinted dark and swept back on his head. He is sitting in the dining room of Burger Castle, a restaurant he started as Hot Dog City on Greene Street, near the Tar River in Greenville, a couple of years ago. He since has opened two more Burger Castles, one in the mall, another in Kinston.

After signing away his name and the right ever to sell 15-cent hamburgers again, Wilber opened a small restaurant, Little Castle, in Greenville. Another drive-in followed, Space House, which grew to two before they failed. In the mid-'60s, Wilber started a chain of little walk-up hot dog and hamburger stands called Little Mint, which grew so quickly in the Carolinas that things got out of control. Wilber resigned as president in 1975 and the chain collapsed.

While he was getting Little Mints going, Hardee's gave up its original building in Greenville after a fire and moved to a new location a few blocks away. Wilber went gleefully back into his old building with a Little Mint. When Little Mints went under, he enlarged the building into a new restaurant, Wilber's Family Favorites, simultaneously opening a big seafood restaurant in Kinston. Both failed and Wilber declared bankruptcy.

He rebounded to start a place called Beef 'N Shakes. "It was ahead of Wendy's," he says, "before they ever got here, square hamburgers and everything."

He opened three of those, then closed two and changed one into a biscuit house, which he sold for enough profit to start Hot Dog City.

Wilber tries not to look back with regret, but he still frets over the contract he signed, even dreams about it. It still bothers him to drive past a Hardee's.

"It's always been pressure on me to see my name up there and I didn't get anything out of it, ain't getting anything from it. I haven't even been recognized since I got out of the company."

At times, while traveling, Wilber has stopped at Hardee's and told people who work in them that he was the one who started the chain. "They come out and shake hands and all that stuff," he says, but he can never be sure if they believe him.

If he hadn't sold out, Wilber might have become as famous as Colonel Sanders, probably would be rich, but he doesn't know if he'd have been able to stay.

"I don't think I'd enjoyed it. You get lost in a company like Hardee's. I don't care who you are, you get lost. My theory is, I like to get out and get things goin', build 10 or 15 stores and sell out. You know what I mean, being a promoter."

"Wilber's a little profit man," says a friend in his presence. "He don't want to wait around for the big profit."

"Yeah," says Wilber, laughing, "give me three or four hundred thousand dollars and let me travel on."

This friend has brought blueprints for Wilber to look at, blueprints of a new restaurant.

"I think the day of the hamburger is not as great as it used to be," Wilber explains. "I think chicken and biscuits and a lot of other things is takin' over. I'm looking at a new chain right now, goina be called Farm House Chicken 'N Biscuits. Built like a farm house. Tin on the roof."

He grins.

"You know it takes people like me to make this world click. Somebody's got to start sumpin'. Hell yeah, I'm gonna keep on doin' it till I die."

The Tobacco Farmer

NASHVILLE   The tobacco by the road is his, not that there is anything to distinguish it from any other tobacco by the side of the old highway, except it hasn't been topped yet.

Tobacco is a common sight in Nash County, nestling right up to the edges of Nashville, a farm town, the county seat. Farm products brought more than $100 million to Nash County last year, nearly half of it from tobacco. Probably a thousand families grow tobacco in the county and many more profit from it. One family that grows it, and has for four generations, is Glen Bass's. A sandy lane west of town leads to his small frame house, which is set back from highway 64A, under a stand of oaks.

"He's barning tobacco," says a neighbor who offers directions to the nearby house of Glen's brother, Clarence, where family members are putting up their third barn of tobacco in two days. This is priming time, the beginning of harvest, begun the day before.

"This is what they call the lugs, or primings," Glen says, taking clumps of pale green tobacco leaves from a long narrow trailer and spreading them on an automatic conveyor leading to the barn door. "This year it's sorta bad. This is just fair. It's small. It drowneded out one time, then got too dry and then it liked to drowneded out again."

This is filler tobacco from the bottom of the stalk. It won't bring much at market.

"I have seen the time when that would sell right good," Glen says, "but they got too choicy now. They want good stuff. In other words, they want B tobacco, top of the stalk. Good stuff."

In nearby fields, hired hands are picking the tobacco and loading it into the trailers that Glen keeps shuttling back and forth from the barn with his tractor.

The barn, covered with corrugated galvanized metal, is tall enough to hang seven tiers of tobacco tied onto sticks. Off two sides of it is a tin-roofed shelter, under which several people are keeping the conveyor fed. Most are family members: Glen's sister, Rachel Barnes; a niece, Kim Baines; a younger brother, Irvin. Only Dorothy Odom, hired by the day, is nonfamily.

Once tobacco was tied onto sticks by hand to be hung in the barn for curing, but now a machine ties it at the end of the conveyor.

"Heap different now," Rachel says. "Used to loop it on a wooden horse, all handwork."

Glen (left) and Mike Bass

Clarence, whose barn this is, and in whose field this tobacco was grown (he has a 5-acre allotment, cut gradually from a high of 13 acres, which he rents to his brother) suffered a heart attack a few years ago and can't work tobacco anymore. He keeps the line supplied with sticks.

"I cut some of these sticks over 30 years ago," he says. "Some of 'em was cut with an ol' Simon, Simon crosscut saw."

Inside the barn, which is only a little cooler than the average sauna, Glen's son, Mike, who's 28, and two teenage nephews, Greg and Shawn Baines, are hanging the sticks of tobacco, sweating as they work, taking turns clambering into the greater heat of the upper levels.

"Yeah, it's about full," Mike says.

This barn will be filled before dinner. Before supper, a fourth nearby barn will be filled, the gas jets on the dirt floor fired to burn a week, by which time the leaves will have dried to a golden brown. Then the tobacco will be removed, taken from the sticks, wrapped in burlap bundles, stored in the packhouse until market time, and these barns will be filled again with more valuable leaves from higher on the stalk.

Glen is not a big tobacco farmer. He and Mike will grow 18 acres this year, all on rented allotments on widely spread fields, and he is worried about some of it. Those patches down by the highway that haven't been topped, for instance.

"We're running behind probably a week or 10 days right now," he says. "We got to get to it, can't get to it. Goin' a have to hire somebody."

Hiring somebody adds to costs, cuts into profits, and when you have to pay out a third of what the tobacco brings just to rent the allotment that allows you to grow it, profits are scant. And that is changing the way Glen looks at tobacco farming.

"Used to like it a lot better than I do today," he says. "Can't make as much money now as you used to. Got you tied down. They freeze our prices and what we buy, they keep going up."

"It's got where it costs more and more to grow, and you don't get no more from it," Mike says.

"Anybody thinks you get rich at it, they ought to try it," Glen says. "You got to plant a whole heap of it to make much at it now. Just barely make a living. That's about it."

Glen's father made a living growing tobacco, raising it with mules. His grandfather grew it, too, although not to the extent his father did. Glen, who's 60, was working in tobacco fields as far back as he can remember. At 19, during World War II, he joined the Marines and was sent off to the Pacific. That might have been his chance to break from tobacco farming, but he came back to it.

"Well," he says, "it's all I knowed."

Now he keeps hearing that the only work he has ever known, the work his father and grandfather did before him, the work his son has taken up, is immoral, that growing tobacco is wrong.

"I reckon that's their belief," he says of people who say that. "They got a right to it."

"They ought to get on somethin' else before they do tobacco," interjects his brother Irvin, who is trying to get the looping machine unjammed.

"I believe I've seen likker kill more people than tobacco," Mike adds.

"I don't say a cigarette don't hurt you," says Glen, who doesn't smoke and hasn't for 30 years, "but you're doing it to yourself. You're not doing it to somebody else. That's an individual thing. Tobacco's something, it's always been here. They going to keep it here. Lot of 'em going to keep smoking it. They going to keep raisin' it. Anybody raisin' it worries, though. I'm getting to where I'm going to be quittin' anyhow. Soon as I can get able to retire, I'll quit."

Will Mike, the only one of Glen's four sons who chose tobacco farming, continue the family tradition?

"I don't know whether he will or not," Glen says. "It's doubtful, the way he keeps talking. I don't know."

"I ain't done nothin' but this all my life," Mike says. "It's all right, just ain't no money in it. Nothin' else to do right now. Anything better comes along, well . . . ."

Stove Hugger Symposium

SPRING HOPE   The group is short this morning. Only three regulars have shown up—carrying Styrofoam cups of steaming coffee from the Showside Grill down the street—to sit around the old coal stove, leaning back in straight-back chairs, considering the affairs of the day.

The judge, for one, is missing, magistrate Stanley Lamb, thus making him a topic of conversation. Nobody can explain his absence.

But the general is here. It's his place, after all. And the writer. And the teacher.

"What this is," says Roy Wilder, the writer, "is an unofficial session of the Sykes Seed Store symposium of stove huggers. We sit around the stove whether it's hot or cold."

He's good with words, Roy is—prides himself on it. Got a book on words coming out this fall—Southern words.

Sykes Store is older than any of these characters, and no doubt has seen many more as odd. It was opened 85 years ago by Bud Sykes, and after he died, his son, Johnny, also called Duck, took over. Johnny died a couple of years ago, and the store fell into the hands of others who didn't fare so well with it. They were about to close the store last year until the general's wife stepped in.

Her name is Beth. She grew up in Spring Hope, loved Sykes Store, couldn't bear to see it close. "It's been here so long," she says. "I think it's unique. You just don't find them like this. We had a man in here yesterday, he said, "This store's just home to me.' He said, 'I used to come in here when I was a little boy.'"

It was Beth who pressured the general to buy the store. It wasn't exactly what he'd pictured himself doing when he retired from the Air Force three years ago, a fighter pilot, commander of the 13th Air Force in the Philippines, Major General J.R. Hildreth. He'd always seen himself with a cushy job in the defense industry. Instead he finds himself worrying about whether he's got enough galvanized washtubs in stock, trying to placate cranky customers who claim the bush bean seeds ain't really bush.

To top it all, the boys call him Cotton because of the color of his hair.

"Some folks call him Whitey," Roy says.

"Mostly, they call him bald," the teacher says.

Not even a general commands proper respect in this crowd.

The teacher's name is Warren Boone, and this morning, as usual, he's barefoot.

Left to right—Cotton Hildreth, the general Roy Wilder, the writer
Warren Boone, the barefoot teacher

"I try to go barefooted some every month," he says. "I can't go
barefooted to school, but I do occasionally slip by with it. I don't
hardly ever put on no more shoes after school's out."

Warren has a master's degree in guidance and teaches agriculture
at Nash County High. He also owns several large farms and raises
corn, chickens, cucumbers, sweet potatoes, tobacco and a few other
things. He rhapsodizes about how it was when he was a boy: plowing
barefoot with a mule, the velvety feel of the fresh furrow under his
foot. He thinks, too, that this need to go barefoot goes back to his
childhood.

"You couldn't go barefooted as long as you wanted to, because
they always tol' you it'd give you a cold. It was after you dug sweet
'taters they wouldn't let you go barefooted no more. I decided when
I got grown and got gone, I'd go barefooted all I wanted to."

He wants to even in snow.

"It ain't too cold," he says. "Had a feller come up to the chicken
house one year, I 'as walkin' around barefooted in the snow. He had
on insulated boots about that thick. He thought that was a curiosity."

Remarkably, he's never suffered any injury from going barefoot,
not even a bee sting.

"Been lucky so far. I ain't never had no trouble with these feet,
never had no corns or nothin'. I think the secret is you learn to walk
easy. You kinda feel your away along. I can walk through most brier
patches, things like that."

Of course, the bottoms of his feet are soiled to the point that scrubbing offers little redemption, but that doesn't bother Warren. "Ain't nobody looks at the bottom of your feet no way."

Nobody ever knows which way the conversation will drift when the regulars gather around the stove each morning.

At these guys' ages, the general says, "there's usually some discussion of the obituary column."

Roy, ever the writer, allows that a sexual adventure might be recalled now and then.

"None of 'em's memories are quite that good," the general says.

This morning nothing important comes up. There is some talk of skinny-dipping in the old baptizing hole, of a barefoot race Warren ran at the town's pumpkin festival, or horticulture ("Cotton likes to mess with flowers and plants," it is explained), and of local personalities.

"When they going to bury the Taylor boys' mother?" Roy asks.

A farmer in overalls comes in and asks Warren, "How much you gittin' for your corn?"

"Ain't got nothin' for it yet," he says.

"Warren gives corn away," Roy says.

"Had one purty good week last year," Warren says. "Give away fourteen hundred ears. Beats sellin' it. Whole lot easier."

The general shows off ancient items from his shelves, a box of Barker's Horse and Cattle Medicinal Powder that he gives to Warren, unsold cans of Bab-O cleanser dating back to World War II, before he is distracted by a potential customer, an out-of-town woman who has just dropped in and tours the store, oohing and aahing as if it were a museum, the general following, politely answering questions.

She leaves without buying anything just as Warren rises and announces, "I reckon I better get on, see if I can get some work done. Somebody got to support this crowd."

"Wash your feet!" the writer calls, as the teacher ambles out the door.

Shirley's Place

RALEIGH   A workday, 5:30 p.m. Eyes need a few moments adjustment from the brightness outside to the smoky dimness within. The music: loud rock. The scent: beery mustiness.

"No services for chains, leathers, colors, pets and weapons in this establishment," warns the sign inside the door, where the $3 cover charge is collected. "Shoes and shirts required."

The after-work crowd is here. Business guys seated by the stage, ties askew, white shirts aglow with black light. Working guys at the bar, hairier, more sturdily dressed, some with names stitched over shirt pockets, keys dangling from belts, protruding wallets hooked with chains.

The dancer onstage, moving jerkily under red lights recessed in the ceiling, is tall and slim, with hair too blonde to be natural. She wears leg warmers and a black leotard cut very high on the sides, exposing bony hips. The leotard is low enough in front to display parts normally covered in public. Aerobics—R-rated.

"Remember," says a voice over the music, "these girls are dancing for tips only." The voice belongs to the DJ in the booth by the door, the collector of entrance fees, the husband of the dancer onstage.

His announcement prompts a stocky young man with a mustache to leave the bar and approach the stage holding out a dollar bill. When the dancer comes near, he tucks the money under the edge of her costume, then takes the tipping stance, hands clasped behind his back, face tilted upward, like a penitent awaiting communion. The dancer leans over, and taking his head in her hands, kisses him deep and long—standard reward for tips, the bigger the bill, the more ardent the kiss.

The whole scene is reflected in the wall of mirrors behind the stage, mirrors with a single word painted broadly in fancy script: "Shirley's."

"I still dance a little bit," says Shirley Everette, the proprietor. "It's fun to be on stage and put on an act. I don't kiss the guys now, though. My dancing days are about over, I guess. I'm 42. I'll dance as long as I can." She laughs. "As long as my looks hold out."

A bit thick in the middle now, Shirley is, but then she was that when she started dancing topless five years ago.

Shirley grew up on a cotton mill hill in Selma, in nearby Johnston County, grew up poor, attending the Baptist church. Shy and soft-spoken, she quit school and got married at 16, had her first baby at 18, her second at 20. She worked in sewing rooms. Her husband, who worked for the railroad, drank.

"Never had any fun," she says. "Workin', cleanin', raisin' kids. That was it."

She forgot fighting. As her husband's drinking grew worse, she decided she couldn't take it anymore, and after 16 years of marriage she took her two sons and left. With no help from her husband, she had to work two jobs at a time to support her children. She was driving a Dolly Madison cake truck and working third shift as a waitress when a friend talked her into entering an amateur topless contest at a Raleigh bar.

"I said, 'I can't do it, I'm too old,'" she recalls. "She said, 'Get over there and try.'"

She can't explain what made her do it, other than the possibility of winning the $100 prize.

"Curiosity, I guess," she says. "Just to see what life was. I'd never been wild, never done anything like that. I thought the guys would laugh me off the stage, but instead they encouraged me."

She didn't win, but she didn't lose either.

"I made more money on tips that night than I could make working two jobs."

That was incentive enough to make her want to become a dancer, but because of her age and weight, she had trouble getting a job. Finally, the owner of another Raleigh bar, the Foxy Lady, gave her a tryout.

"He didn't think I'd make any money, but I ended up making better tips than the pretty girls. I wasn't stuck on myself and I enjoyed dancing. That's the secret to this business."

Shortly after she started dancing, she quit both her previous jobs. She was working fewer hours, making far more money than she'd ever made, and having a good time.

Then she got married again and quit dancing to have another baby. But four months after her son, Dougie, was born, she was dancing again, this time at a small bar on U.S. 64 east called the Klassy Kat. Late in 1980, she bought the bar, expanded it into another building, and opened it in 1981 as Shirley's. She since has had another baby, her first daughter, now a year old, and opened another business, Dougie's, a sexy apparel shop, in a former wallpaper outlet next to the bar.

She brings the children with her to the shop each morning, takes them to a baby sitter in late afternoon when business at the bar picks up.

"I got lonesome after the big ones got grown," she says of the children. "I'm not happy unless I'm fussin' or busy."

Busy she stays, much of her energy going to mother her dancers. There are six now, Misty, Debbie, Nancy, Tabitha, Karen and Holly, ranging in age from 18 to 28, only one married, but the help-wanted sign stays out, and the line-up varies regularly.

"You're their mother, their psychiatrist, their doctor," Shirley says with a sigh. "You're never their boss. You're just a lot of little things rolled into one. They all got personal problems and they bring them to work.

"You got young ladies who sometimes are hard-headed. They won't listen to their mother. They going to do what they want to. When a guy tells 'em one thing and you tell 'em another, they don't believe you. They all want to be wanted and needed and loved, but what they don't understand nine times out of 10 is they got to make sure that guy is right for 'em. They're in love with the idea of love. That's what happens."

For her girls, as Shirley calls them, she has rules. No prostitution. No drugs. No drinking on the job. No dating customers.

"I always find out about everything they do," she says. "My girls know that if they go off with a guy, I fire 'em. You got girls who don't realize they can make a lot of money by dancing only. They let guys turn their heads. Lot of these girls quit school, don't have any training, and they make $500 to $800 a week. A girl can make more money dancing topless, not doing anything but dancing topless, than she can at any job she goes at after high school."

There are rules for the customers, too. No drunkenness, rowdiness or vulgarity. No laying of hands upon the dancers, who circulate in the bar when they aren't dancing. The rules, the cover charge and the $1.25 price of beer are Shirley's way of keeping out the riff-raff, but it doesn't always work. There have been fights and a few serious incidents.

One night two toughs came in, fresh from pushing a guy's face into a meat grinder at a pizza house, and pounced upon a hapless patron who brushed against one of them. They were pounding his head with beer bottles when Shirley's son got an unloaded rifle and tried to stop them, but they took away the rifle and hit him with it before fleeing, taking the rifle with them.

Another night, an infuriated customer ejected for slapping his girlfriend, ran down Shirley's husband, David, with a car in the parking lot, leaving him in a coma for two days but without serious permanent injuries.

These things worry Shirley not only because of people getting hurt but because it gives her place a bad name and leads some people to believe that her profession is less than respectable.

"What I want to do, I want to make topless dancing a little bit more high classed and acceptable," she says. "Sally Rand and Gypsy Rose Lee, they made society accept burlesque. That's the same thing. If a dancer gets up there and acts like a slut, she's going to be a slut. If she gets up there and acts like a lady, she's going to be a lady. I know some secretaries that are not very ladylike at times.

"You can see more nudity at the movies, at the beaches, you name it, than you can here.

"I still intend one way or the other, before I go out of this business to show people you can make an honest job like topless dancing honest. To put somebody down before you know the circumstances and know what it's all about is just the wrong thing to do.

"Don't you think anybody has a right to live their life the way they want to as long as they don't hurt anybody else? That's my motto. As long as you don't hurt anybody, you've got the right to live like you want to whether anybody else approves of you or not.

"I like myself, because I try to help people. I try to help any girl who needs help. I've given people money that needed it. I'm not getting rich but I could if I used other people, if I just looked after myself instead of falling for all the sob stories I hear. I've encouraged girls to go back to school, to learn and get a business for their self sometime. Even though I run a bar, I've still got morals."

Passage

Five miles from where U.S. 64 parts company with U.S. 1, west of Raleigh, it widens to four lanes to pass what once was its most deadly spot.

For years the junction with N.C. 55 showed up in the annual list of the state's 10 most dangerous intersections. Dozens died here before the state widened 64 and built an overpass for 55. Now traffic zips by unmindful of the spot's bloody past.

Just beyond the intersection, on a hill overlooking it, two signs tell a story of a failed dream. The signs stand in front of an old farm, the yellow-painted, tin-roofed house set back from the road. In front of the house, an old barn has been partially transformed in artful fashion. Clearly, it was going to be a studio, with half-octagon skylights, an unusual and pretty building, but construction stopped, unfinished. "Art Farm," says one sign in fading letters painted with a flourish. "For Sale," says a newer sign, bigger and more business-like, erected by a real estate company.

Boats are a familiar sight on this part of the highway. B. Everett Jordan Lake lies ahead, and since its opening two years ago, it has had a great effect on the road. Traffic has increased, particularly on weekends, and new convenience marts abound to serve lake visitors. Signs offer crickets and minnows and fishing tackle. Jordan Lake Marine, a boat shop, is miles from the lake itself.

Jordan Lake, which covers 14,300 acres, is the largest body of fresh water along the highway, and as if in recognition of this distinction, the highway widens again to four lanes to cross it. Two miles of causeway and bridges carry the highway through the lake's center, offering a scenic view that was not so scenic until two years ago.

Environmental concerns and construction problems kept the lake from being filled for years after its bed was cleared, and the view from the highway was of mud holes, weeds and scrub growth, crisscrossed with ruts left by trail bikes.

Now the only trails visible are temporary, the wakes left by boats of many descriptions, hundreds of them on weekends, dozens on weekdays. On the north side of the causeway, another trail can be seen, the old highway, dipping in and out of the lake.

Five miles west of the lake, the highway crosses one of the two rivers that feed it, the Haw, (the other is the New Hope) shallow and rocky and orange with sediment, before it begins to climb again toward Pittsboro, county seat of Chatham County.

Circle City, the CBers call Pittsboro, because all highways leading into the town—U.S. highways 64, 15-501 and N.C. 87, converge in a circle around the old courthouse which sits squarely in the center of U.S. 64, guarded by the statue of a Confederate soldier on a pedestal, permanently vigilant, facing northward.

The highway is at its worst between Pittsboro and Siler City, the pavement uneven, patched and potholed, with shoulders too narrow to accommodate even a small car—a country road accommodating city highway traffic. A motorist with the misfortune of a flat tire could be in trouble.

The land is hillier now, and in spots, the highway is cut between steep banks covered with scrub growth and kudzu. At other points sharp dropoffs are unprotected by guardrails.

This is pulpwood and livestock country, the rich red dirt growing tall pines to feed the pulp mills and tall corn and grass to feed dairy cows, beef cattle and quarter horses. In some green fields, great rolls of freshly cut hay lie browning in the sun.

A sign offers chair caning and basket making at a house on a hill; a roadside trailer boasts a pig lot out back.

Siler City welcomes travelers from the east with the unpleasant aromas of the Rocky River. On the west, two huge U.S. flags employed as advertising gimmicks by competing convenience stores on opposite sides of the highway, wave goodbye.

Five miles out of Siler City, the highway passes into Randolph County, and after six more miles into Ramseur, a river mill town, where a movie, "Killers Three," once was filmed and where an old railroad depot has been restored next to the highway with a small section of isolated track barren of any railroad car. West of town the highway crosses the Deep River, sluggish here, held back by the mill dam just downstream.

At a business complex halfway between Ramseur and Asheboro, a sign at a used car lot attracts great attention. "Don't Rent A Wreck, Buy One At Shoddy Sales," it says on one side. On the other side, it employs a term not acceptable in polite company. "We Finance The S____ Cars In The South."

Yet another sign, this one in the window at Hodgin Flower Shop, a little farther along the highway, tells a whole story with a single word: "Retired."

Not until it approaches Asheboro does the winding highway seem that it is nearing mountains, but that is indeed the case. Asheboro, highest spot along the highway to this point (part of it is nearly 1,000 feet above sea level), lies in the northeastern edge of the Uwharrie Mountains, believed by many geologists to be the oldest mountains in North America, some of the oldest in the world. Once, hundreds of millions of years ago, they towered more than 20,000 feet. Now few reach 1,000 feet, but several of those peaks are visible from the highway, as it traverses the northern rim of the range, heading toward younger mountains that make the Uwharries look like mere hills.

The Boy Who Went Across the Road

SILER CITY   Most people passing on the highway probably never notice the old house, although it is close by the roadside. It's almost hidden from view by the hedges that engulf it, growing above its rusty roof, hiding the gray, collapsing boards of its never-painted walls.

"Ol' house is give out," she says.

She hasn't been inside it in years.

"Ol' place like that, you don't know what's liable to be in there. I just don't go in there unless somebody goes with me. Could be a snake get after me."

She spent nearly 25 years in the house before abandoning it to live in the brick store her husband was building next door. The house was old when she moved into it nearly half a century ago, a little farm house on a hill, back from the road. When she and her husband bought the farm, he decided he wanted the house closer to the road.

"He took a horse and got a sawmill man to help him drag it down here," she recalls. "Rolled it on logs, pulled it with a ol' white horse. They drug it from on top the hill. Wasn't no shade here, so I went on top the hill and dug up them hedges and put 'em out there. I love shade but I couldn't keep 'em cut. It was a purty place, but my husband never did work on it, didn't keep it up. It just give out."

The store, equipped with living quarters, not only solved the house problem but another as well.

"We had a crippled boy that went across the road. He loved to go set in that store up yonder. He was going to get killed going across the road, so my husband, he just built this thing so he wouldn't have to go across the road, and he hasn't crossed the road now in I don't know how many years."

The store, named for the boy (she doesn't want names used: "Just don't like to have my name in public," she says), never amounted to much as a store. Her husband never finished it for one thing. One end is still without windows, still incomplete inside. Her husband got so he couldn't work, and they closed the store before his death 11 years ago. But she still sold a little gas until recent years. The pumps are still by the front door, still functional, and she hasn't given up the idea that she might sell gas again.

"I could get some now, I reckon," she says. "I still got the license."

But she knows that more than likely the pumps will be like the old pickup truck, overgrown with weeds and vines, sitting by the

105

house. Her son once drove that truck a little and she never sold it because he thought he might drive it again someday.

He was born with a problem in his legs, and once he went to a hospital where doctors said the problem could be corrected, but the boy cried, didn't want to stay and his daddy brought him back home.

"He wouldn't never take him back," she says. "He loved home so good that he wouldn't make him go."

The boy never left home again.

"He went to school a little but he couldn't learn," she says.

For a while he got so that he could drive the truck and tractor around the farm and help his dad with odd jobs, but in recent years he has rarely ventured beyond the front door.

He is 52 now, bent and pale, with a white beard. "He can't walk too good and he can't see too good," she says. "He likes the television—he did till he got where he couldn't see good—and he likes the air conditioning. He's right smart nervous. He couldn't live by hisself."

She has devoted her life to his, and that means she rarely gets out herself anymore, other than to cut the grass, tend her dogs or sit in a lawn chair by the gas pumps watching the traffic pass only a few yards away.

"I used to love to drive," she says, watching the steady stream of cars and big trucks. "Used to be, driving a car or riding was pure pleasure to me. Now I don't care about it because of all these wrecks. That knocks the pleasure out of it.

"Used to, when I was proud, I wanted me a big car, but all that's gone out of me now. I just want to be comfortable. I tell you what, I put my stomach before I do most things.

"I spend my days a' cookin'. We both got a big appetite. I'd spend the last cent I got to get what I want to eat. My appetite rules me." She laughs. "Don't I look like it? I like cured meat. Can't stand fresh meat. Don't want no hamburger. I don't like to eat out, don't like a thing I can find out."

She has no trouble getting what she needs. Neighbors keep a watch on her. One, who works at a supermarket in town, calls every day to see if she wants him to bring her anything.

"I got the best neighbors in the world," she says. "That's one reason I don't want to leave down here."

Leaving is a subject that has come up before. She owns a duplex apartment in town that she rents, and some have suggested that she might be more comfortable there where things are more convenient.

"I like it out here in the country," she says. "Everybody likes home, don't they? I've lived here all this time. I like my dogs. I'd be afraid to have my dogs in town. I don't care nothin' about town no how."

She has only four dogs now, all mongrels, but there have been more. Two are tied by the front door, two live inside, where visitors are rarely invited. Three of the dogs are descendants of a female stray she took in 45 years ago. The other is a stray that showed up a couple of years back.

"He come here about perished to death," she says. "Wasn't nothin' but a stack of bones. Poor little pitiful thing couldn't hardly walk. I love anything that's got life in it. This one, I have to scratch his back. He wants you to rub his back. You go out there and he'll 'bout knock you down to get you to rub his back. He wouldn't bite a snake, but he acts like it, don't you purty boy?"

"I may not have much," she says, reaching to rub the eager dog's back, "but I try to be happy with whatever that comes. That's what I do now, just try to live from day to day."

The Smell of Cedar

RAMSEUR   Once he worked right through the summer, swelter-
ing in the old tin building, the big fans stirring the dust.

No more.

Now he shuts down in July and August. The machines are quiet,
the fans still, and the red dust lies settled over everything, inches
deep in spots, the accumulation of decades. But the aroma cannot
be idled. It overwhelms the air inside the dark building, a unique
aroma, unmistakable: cedar.

"I smell a little bit of it on Monday morning," Wade Wright says,
"but after that I don't smell it much."

He has become as accustomed to the aroma as he has to the feel
of the wood that produces it, and he loves both.

"It's not a perfect wood," he says. "It's between a soft and a hard
wood. It's harder than most people think it is, especially close to
the heart. It's just an odd wood. It's hard to dress, to get it real
smooth. You got to dress it just right or it'll jerk out around the knots."

He's paid a price for loving such an imperfect wood, and he raises
first his left hand, then his right, to show it.

"I lost that one before I got married," he says, indicating the missing
middle finger of his left hand. "When I was about 17. On a jointer."

The tip of another finger on that hand went 12 years ago, the
thumb on his right hand six years later.

"A knot broke off under my thumb and my thumb went in," he
says. "All of 'em on the same machine."

In the old building he shows off the offending machine, which,
like all the other machinery in this plant, is as old or older than the
building itself, some of it originally designed to operate with pedals
and hand cranks.

"We started off with gasoline engines for power here," says Wade.
"We'd run a belt from the gasoline engine to this line shaft here and
run our machines off the line shaft."

That was in 1936, and Wright's Cedar Furniture and Cabinet Works
had just moved from Asheboro onto U.S. 64, west of Ramseur. Wade
was 15 then and he'd quit school in the 9th grade to help his daddy
in his business.

His father, Edgar, had worked in a cabinet shop and a casket
factory in Asheboro before opening a small woodworking shop at
his home in 1921, the year Wade was born.

"He made ice boxes and screen windows, mantles, most anything
that came along," Wade recalls.

108

After a few years, Edgar built a shop on Salisbury Street, a crude building covered with corrugated metal. When he decided to move the shop so that more people might see what he made, he and his sons dismantled the building and reassembled it on the highway. By then Edgar had begun specializing in cedar cabinets and furniture.

World War II took Wade away from the shop, but after the war, he returned to it along with his younger brother, Bernard. "That's all I knew, really," he says. "It's something you get into it and you just stay in it until you get ready to quit."

Yet, he acknowledges that he might not have been able to stay in it if his wife, Doris, hadn't worked at the GE plant in Asheboro, especially as the children were growing up. Furniture making was slow and tedious. A person could turn out only so much a week, and the Wrights never believed in charging outlandish prices. Wade never made much money.

"It wasn't a real good living," he says.

"I'd rather he'd been in that than anything else, though," says Doris, "because he liked it."

They never had many luxuries, but rarely suffered want. They started in a two-room house that they built next to his daddy's house, which was next to the plant, and added to it gradually as their three children came, and now it is a comfortable brick house that serves them well, furnished with furniture that Wade made.

"It's not the money you have, it's how you take care of what you have," says Doris.

Wade's father, who was still working at age 75, died in 1961, and after his death, Wade and his brother kept the plant operating. But after his brother died in 1972, Wade faced the prospect of hiring somebody to help him, which would have been unprofitable, or closing down. That's when Doris quit her job to help him.

"I do a lot of little things," she says, "sanding, glueing. It's a lot of handwork, a lot of handwork. I love it. The more you're in it, the more it grows on you."

Wade loved making chests, had been specializing in that for years, and after his brother's death, the plant turned out no more bedroom furniture, wardrobes or cabinets, only chests. He and Doris can make three standard-size chests a week, fewer if they are bigger or more complicated. They sell them retail at the plant. The simplest sells for $147, the most expensive for $211. The only advertising they've ever done is to put a couple of chests in the window of the concrete block display building at the plant.

"We sell to people all over the United States," says Doris. "We've got chests in England, Hawaii . . ."

". . . Canada, France," adds Wade.

They usually have a three-month backlog of orders. But that doesn't keep Wade from closing down in the heat of summer and again in January and February, when the old buildings are so hard to heat.

He's 63 now and he just doesn't feel up to working the way he once did. He has no plans for quitting. He loves too much the feel and smell and challenge of the wood.

"Every piece of it's different," he says, "and it's an enjoyment to see how it turns out."

Yet he knows that the time will come when he may no longer want, or be able, to make his chests. What will happen to the plant then, he isn't sure.

His own two sons were allergic to cedar dust and never able to help him at his work. One became a mortician, the other a meat cutter. He thinks he's probably the end of the line of Wrights and cedar.

"Unless these boys want to suffer it out and work in it some, I guess it'll just close down," he says. "Might sell it, but I don't know if I could or not. You got to like something like this to want to do it."

The Refugees

ASHEBORO   The day the rocket fell near his house was the day Henry Tan decided the time had come to leave Phnom Penh.

It was late in 1971. The war in Vietnam and Laos had spilled into Cambodia, and things were looking bad in the capital. So Henry, an English teacher of Chinese ancestry, decided to move his family. Henry was from a family of means. His father was a prominent import-export merchant who had relatives and business contacts in Hong Kong and Singapore. Children of other educated, well-to-do Cambodian families studied French, but Henry's father gave his children Anglo names and insisted they learn English. When Henry was a teenager his father sent him to study in Singapore.

As the war grew worse, Henry pooled his resources and moved his wife, Ma Li, and son, William, to the town of Pai Lin in the mountains on the border with Thailand. There, he bought a plantation which grew mangos and other tropical fruits. The land also bore fruit of another kind—sapphires and rubies—and Henry hired workers to dig them for him.

"That place," says Henry, "was very peaceful."

For four years, his family thrived, but war eventually reached the mountains, too. And in 1975, as Cambodia was falling, and communist troops were approaching Pai Lin, Henry knew what he must do. He put his family in his Jeep—there were four of them now; Ma Li had just had another son, Telap—and drove them to the jungle river that separated Cambodia from Thailand. Carrying the children, a single bag of clothing, what money they had been able to get their hands on, and a small bag of their best rubies and sapphires, Henry and Ma Li waded chest-deep to freedom. Henry never had any doubts that he was doing the right thing.

"Many, many people, because of their property, they think if they go they got nothing, and in the other country living is high, how can they live on nothing?" he said. "They didn't want to go so they stay and they got caught by the communists and killed. We just got away. We don't know what going to happen next."

What happened was that they made their way to a refugee camp at a U.S. Air Force base where they remained for a few months before being flown to another camp in Arkansas. There, Vietnamese officials in charge of the camp stole their money and jewels, which never were recovered. There, too, they learned that groups or individuals from five places had offered to sponsor them in their new home. They could choose from New York, Los Angeles, Seattle,

111

Marie and Henry Tan

Temple, Texas, or a place they'd never heard of, Asheboro, North Carolina. The immigration official who gave them this news was a woman who'd worked 38 years in Peking.

"She could talk Mandarin better than we could," says Henry. "She said among these five cities, Asheboro is a very good small town to raise a family, not very cold, not very hot. We had little baby, four months old. I told her we don't like to live in big city. So she give us Asheboro. She said, 'Asheboro is very good.'"

Henry had $30 when he arrived in Asheboro on Sept. 12, 1975, but the five churches that sponsored his family left him no need to worry. They had rented a house, furnished it, brought in lots of food, even had a job for Henry.

"The churches arranged everything very, very good," says Henry. "The house is 100 times better than we have in Cambodia. Everything prepared so good when we arrived. We were very excited and very happy."

On the third day after his arrival, Henry awoke with a cold and fever, but he still walked a half mile to his new job operating a knitting machine at a textile plant. He continued to walk for a month until his sponsors got him a car, a '68 Pontiac. By the third month, Henry was paying his own rent, making his own way.

A year and a half after his arrival, Henry decided to save money by renting a smaller, cheaper house. He also got a better job at another textile mill, cleaning machines.

During his third year in Asheboro, Henry and his family were invited to celebrate Chinese New Year in Greensboro with a group of area people of Chinese ancestry. There he met a man who was a cook in a Chinese restaurant. The man could speak no English, but he wanted to start his own restaurant. He tried to talk Henry into becoming a partner with him.

The idea intrigued Henry, but he knew nothing about the restaurant business. His friend said it would be easy to learn. So after three years in textile mills, Henry quit his job and went to work at a Chinese restaurant in Cary, near Raleigh, where his friend had become chief cook.

"First day, I washing dishes, first job," Henry says with a laugh. "Second day, chopping vegetables and meat, learn to be fourth cook's job."

Soon, he became a waiter. He worked there four months, coming home only one day a week, living the rest of the time in an apartment with other restaurant employees.

When a new Chinese restaurant opened in High Point, Henry got a job there as waiter, enabling him to move back home. By that time he'd decided his friend in Cary was too temperamental to join in a partnership, but he still wanted to have his own restaurant. Soon, he was manager of the High Point restaurant, and after four months, he decided the time had come to start his own. In Asheboro.

His friends and sponsors were worried. Asheboro was not the kind of town that took easily to new and foreign things. Pizza had trouble getting a foothold in Asheboro.

"My sponsor scared to death," Henry says. "He was so worried that I would have to close my business and be very bad in debt. We have to think of the good side and the bad side. If I couldn't make the business go, then I have to go back to the factory and work two jobs and pay back everybody I owe."

Without established credit, Henry couldn't get a loan from a bank, but he got small loans from friends in several parts of the country. And in July, 1978, he and his wife—who was now called Marie, because an immigration official had written her name that way when she arrived in the country—opened Bamboo Gardens Oriental Restaurant in a failed barbecue stand on the side of U.S. 64.

The place was jammed for the first month, but Henry heard some complaints. "What kind of a cafe don't have bread?" one man demanded to know. Others said that vegetables weren't cooked completely and dishes were too spicy. One customer reported them to the health department after Marie, who still didn't speak English well, was misunderstood to say cat meat instead of crab meat when describing the ingredients of a dish.

But overall, reception was good and Henry and Marie were happy. Until the second month. Then business dropped drastically.

"I don't worry," Henry says, recalling his reaction. "I just try all my best to do my duty. Slow days, I try to prepare to do good when busy."

Business began to grow in the third month, and it has remained good since. The restaurant is open six days a week, and Henry and Marie work 12 hours each day. On the seventh day, they often can be found at the restaurant, too, doing work they can't get done on the other days.

But the work has paid off. "Here," says Henry, "if you work hard, you make a good living."

They now have their own brick house with three bedrooms. They have many luxuries. Marie drives a new Buick. Henry just bought himself a new Chevrolet Blazer. They are saving money to send their children to college.

And the children have adapted well.

"They love everything here," says Henry. "The smaller boy, he doesn't eat our food. Only chicken chow mein and wonton soup. All the time he wants hamburgers, steak, pizza, hot dogs. He grows too big. He's nine years old and weighs 135 pounds."

Because of their success, Henry and Marie have been able to help other refugees, among them Marie's family. For years, they worried about the families they left in Cambodia, now Kampuchea. Henry never heard from his family and assumes that his parents, his brother and sister were killed. Marie, who came from a family of 12 brothers and sisters, discovered that her family was being held in death camps, and she sent money to hire mercenary soldiers to free them. Her father and four of her brothers and sisters and their families were killed in the camps, but her mother and the remainder of her brothers and sisters and their families escaped, surviving on roots and rain water, and eventually arrived in Asheboro for a joyous reunion in 1981.

That was the happiest day for Henry and Marie since they had arrived in Asheboro, but their proudest day came two years ago in Greensboro when they became United States citizens.

"We feel it's too wonderful for us to be a great country's citizen," says Henry. "Because everything in this country is so good, so great, the culture, the laws, the human rights, the freedom. That's why so many people in the other countries love this country more than the American citizens do.

"Sometimes I just go drive. When I drive to anywhere in this country, I like to watch the scenery, beautiful scenery, beautiful road, beautiful trees, especially in the fall and spring, changing colors, so beautiful. I feel so happy watching all these beautiful places on the road, so clean. What a beautiful, wonderful country, I think. How wonderful for me to be here."

Sid Weaver's Legacy

LEXINGTON   In its first 300 miles, U.S. 64 is not exactly a gastronomic delight. Even the state's native dish, barbecue, is meagerly represented.

Nearly 200 miles of highway pass before the first wood-cooked barbecue is reached at Smith's Bar-B-Q in Knightdale, east of Raleigh. In the next 100 miles, the highway passes only one other wood-fired barbecue stand, the Blue Mist, east of Asheboro. Then it reaches Lexington and hits the mother lode.

Lexington is to barbecue as High Point is to furniture, as Raleigh is to politics, as Chapel Hill is beer drinking. It is the center of the action, a bastion of tradition.

The Yellow Pages of the Lexington telephone book list 19 barbecue places. This for a town of fewer than 16,000 people. By contrast, Charlotte, a city with more than 20 times Lexington's population, can count its barbecue places on one hand.

Two basic styles of barbecue are found in North Carolina. One is called Eastern, usually found east of Raleigh, a style that largely has given up tradition. The other is called Lexington, because it was from this town that it spread across the Piedmont, taking tradition with it.

You need only drive into Lexington to get a whiff of that tradition, for the pungent aroma of pork cooking slowly over hickory coals still enriches the town's air, just as it has for more than half a century.

"When I was just a kid we'd go to town in the wagon," says J.B. Tarlton, who because of his girth is known as Big Jay. "You could smell that barbecue a-cookin' half a mile away. When the country people or anybody came to Lexington you had to have a barbecue when you smelled that. You couldn't go home without one. They were 10 cents apiece. My daddy'd tie the mules up at ol' Grimes Mill lot back there, and we'd go to Uncle Sid's tent."

Uncle Sid Weaver: He was the daddy of Lexington barbecue, although there are some who say that honor should be shared by Jess Swicegood. Uncle Sid was a farmer who lived south of town. A niece who grew up in his house, Willie Harris, remembers hearing family stories about how he started cooking barbecue while tending curing fires at his tobacco barns.

Word got around about Uncle Sid's barbecue, and people started asking him to cook for them on special occasions. His barbecue became so popular that sometime in the '20s he began selling it from a tent on a city-owned lot near the courthouse on weekends and court days.

Wayne Monk

Big Jay can still see that tent with its counter and wooden benches, the soft drink box with the big hunks of ice in it, the copper bun steamer, the fat squat trunk of an oak tree that served as a chopping block, still can see Uncle Sid, cleaver in hand, chopping the barbecue he cooked in a pit in the ground behind the tent.

"Never saw him when he wasn't smilin'," Big Jay says. "He was always wearin' his apron and a white cafe hat and chewin' his tobaccer. Juice'd run out of each corner of his mouth while he was fixin' you a barbecue."

116

Years later, just as Uncle Sid was getting ready to move out of his tent into a dirt-floored cement block building on the same site, Big Jay went to work for Uncle Sid. That was in the Depression. Uncle Sid was in his 70s then. B.J., who was a long way from becoming Big Jay, was a slim 22, married a year and desperately in need of a job.

"Back in those days, you took a job anywhere you could," he says, "and I was offered the job there for $7 a week, seven days a week. The first morning I went to work, Uncle Sid hired two boys, another boy and myself. He handed me an ol' kraut cutter, slaw cutter, just a little bitty ol' thing, and around at the back was an ol' stock room. He told me to go around there and cut slaw. He gave the other boy a box of salt and a box of black pepper and told him to fill the salt and pepper shakers. About 30 minutes later, he came back to see how we was doin'. I was standing up over a tub of slaw cutting the cabbage. He said, 'You're doin' fine.' The other boy was settin' down fillin' up the salt and pepper shakers, and he run him off right then.

"Uncle Sid, the next mornin', he put me to cookin' meat. 'Course he stayed with me all the time, showed me when to fire it and how and all."

Big Jay credits Uncle Sid with creating the Lexington style, which is cooking only shoulders instead of split pigs, as is done in the East, serving the meat with a thin sweet-and-sour sauce made of water, vinegar, sugar, catsup, salt and pepper, as opposed to the stronger vinegar-hot pepper sauce of the East. The heated sauce was called dip because a little mop was used to dip into it and splash it on the meat. The meat was served with a red slaw made from a recipe similar to the dip—cabbage, vinegar, sugar, catsup, salt and pepper.

Uncle Sid's sister-in-law, Dell Yarborough, mother of Willie Harris, created the dip and the sauce, Big Jay maintains, but Willie says that her aunt Virge, Uncle Sid's wife, also had a hand in it.

Not long after Uncle Sid taught Big Jay to cook barbecue, he moved into his new building with an above-ground brick pit out back, and soon after that he sold his business to Alton Beck and retired to his farm.

"When Alton Beck bought it, he didn't know nothing about barbecue," Big Jay says. "He sold shoe polish for Griffin Shoe Polish Company."

Big Jay helped teach him the business and became his assistant manager. In 1951, two years after Uncle Sid's death, Big Jay bought Taylor's Drive-In, which he and his wife, Stamey, operated for 10 years before opening a new place on Highway 8, Tarlton's Barbecue.

A lot of people who worked for Uncle Sid and Alton Beck went on to start their own barbecue places in Lexington and other towns. The same was true for those who worked for Uncle Sid's chief competitor, Jess Swicegood. Jess sold his place to Warner Stamey and started another barbecue stand in Winston-Salem before his death, at 56, in 1942. Warner Stamey later sold his place and started another in Greensboro. Men who worked for Stamey started places all over the Piedmont.

"It was all just like a big family a-springin' out every which a-way," says Big Jay, who at 67 has been retired and confined to a wheelchair for 13 years.

Wherever Lexington-style barbecue spread, so did the tradition of cooking over hardwood, hickory as much as possible. In recent years, that tradition has been tainted by electric cookers. Even a few places in Lexington have installed them.

Wayne Monk doesn't think the tradition is threatened, though. He is the town's most famous barbecue man. Last summer, he cooked for President Reagan and other heads of state at the summit conference in Williamsburg, Va. His place, Lexington Barbecue #1, on U.S. 64, has been hailed as one of America's best barbecue houses by Craig Claiborne of the New York Times, among other authorities.

A student of Warner Stamey, Wayne still does things much as Jess Swicegood and Sid Weaver did them.

"You have to," he says. "I guess it's just imbedded in the people of this area what good barbecue is, and they demand it. There's still a lot of pride, too. I don't want to change anything. This is the way I want to do it, and I hope my son will want to do it. I'm sure he will. I've got one son and two son-in-laws here, and I'm sure they'll stay in the business for years to come. So it's going to be here. We're proud of it."

The Oldest Policeman

MOCKSVILLE   It's been months since he was able to walk his beat. In the little green house facing William Street, a few feet off U.S. 64, Avery Foster still puts on his uniform now and then—just for the feel of it.

It doesn't fit well anymore. He has grown so frail that without suspenders he probably wouldn't be able to keep the pants up. But he's proud of it anyway, proud of the handcuffs on his belt, proud of the .38 special on his hip, proud of the U.S. flag on the right shoulder of his shirt and the patch on the left shoulder that says Mocksville Police Department.

"They say I'm the oldest one in the state," he says. "I don't know."

It seems unlikely that any other town would have a policeman still on active duty at age 89, but Mr. Avery, as he is known around Mocksville, doesn't think that's so special.

"I like to work," he says, "and they need me. I've always worked, and I just wanted to work. Been workin' since I was 10 years old. Ain't never made anything but I just worked."

At 10 he became a house boy for a prominent local family. His mother worked for the family as a maid, his father as a yard man. As a teenager, he went to work as a delivery boy at the general store owned by the family. There he remained doing various jobs until the store went out of business in 1969 when he was 74.

That was when Mr. Avery became a full-time policeman. He was experienced in police work. He'd been doing it part-time for 24 years.

In 1945, Mocksville had only two policemen, both white, and a problem in the black section along Depot Street. The town board turned to Avery to resolve the problem.

"Some of the boys was a little rough up here on the street, and they asked me to take care of it," he says.

They granted him police powers and a badge but no uniform or pistol and sent him out to try to stop the drinking, cussing, fighting and dice shooting that was taking place every night.

"The first day I worked was a picnic day," he remembers. "Everybody thought that was just a one-day job when I went there."

He made his first arrest that day—a man who'd tried to cut another man with a knife and succeeded only in cutting his pants.

If there were those who thought Avery Foster wouldn't be back and didn't mean business, they soon discovered the error of their judgment. He was back every night.

119

"When I started, I had a job, I mean a *job*," he says. "Just kept me busy, but they found out I'd do it, I'd lock 'em up, and it slowed down some."

By the end of his first year, he'd been issued a uniform and weapons, and he'd begun to gain respect on the street. He tried to present an image of being tough but fair, and he wanted people to know that he would do his job no matter what.

"I had a friend I run with and I arrested his son, and he tried to get a fellow to kill me. I locked his son up two or three times. I'd lock my own up, didn't make no difference to me. I got a son that I locked up twice. If they done wrong, I'd lock 'em up. That's what I was supposed to do, and I just went ahead and done it."

Rarely did he have trouble making arrests, and never did he get hurt. Only once did he use his pistol, and he doesn't like to recall that. He was trying to arrest a man on the railroad tracks.

"He decided he wanted my blackjack, and I didn't know whether they wanted me to give it to him or not. We settled it right there. Let's just don't talk about that."

He'd rather talk about the thieves he caught by hiding in stores at night, or how he once learned who had stolen a hundred-dollar bill from an old man's house just by finding out who was spending money extravagantly and confronting him.

In his early years, it was profitable for him to catch criminals. He was paid on a fee basis. "Like if I arrest you, I got three dollars, and if I locked you up I got four. See I was kinda careful on that because they would think you was arresting them for the money." He's been on salary since becoming a full-time patrolman in 1969.

In recent years, Mr. Avery has walked the downtown beat. He drives his own car to work and parks in front of the Davie County Courthouse. "You know that spot that says no parking?" he says with a gold-toothed grin. "That's mine."

He checks in at every store and stops to talk with people on the street. He hasn't chased down a troublemaker in years, and it's been a long time since he locked anybody up. His last arrest, a year or so ago, was for speeding.

"Mostly, I just write parking tickets and things like that," he says. "Try to get out of going to court."

Mr. Avery got sick last October. December was the last time he was able to work. He's had pneumonia twice since then and has lost a lot of weight, but the police department has kept him on the payroll and let him know that his job is there if he can come back.

"I tell you, I don't know," Mr. Avery says. "The doctor says I worked enough. He says I ought to set down and let somebody else do it. I like to work. If I get so I can walk good, I'm goin' back. Yessir, if I can walk, I'll be back."

Passage

Two miles west of Mocksville, at Bear Creek, U.S. 64 passes through historic land.

In 1753, Lord Granville, one of North Carolina's eight lords proprietors, granted 640 acres along Bear Creek to Squire Boone, who had moved his family to North Carolina from Pennsylvania. There he built a log cabin. One of his children, Daniel, then 19, became a hunter, killing as many as 30 deer a day for their hides and selling the hides to a buckskin pants plant in Salisbury.

Daniel remained in Davie County for nearly 10 years, married there, started a family and bought his father's land in 1759. Five years later, he moved his family to Wilkes County. Ever restless, he moved again in 1773, blazing the Wilderness Trail into Kentucky and his name into history books.

Today, Daniel Boone's former land is cornfield and pasture. The only indication that it ever was his is a state historic marker by the side of the highway. Not far from the highway, Daniel's parents lie buried in Joppa Cemetery.

Just beyond the Boone land the highway has the first of a series of encounters with Interstate 40. Here it changes character again. For the next 70 miles, the interstate assumes its burden of traffic, turning U.S. 64 into a country road traveled by infrequent cars and pickup trucks, rarely by tractor-trailers.

This is rolling farmland, green with pasture, soybeans and corn. Cows huddle under trees seeking relief from midday heat. Sunflowers bow their heads in gardens of brick farmhouses and signs in front yards offer sweet corn and tomatoes for sale. One barn bears on its roof a faded message once familiar throughout North Carolina, "See Rock City."

Eight miles after it first crosses over I-40, the highway loops back under it, then loops back again nine miles later, creating a dollar sign on the map. At the center of the dollar sign, Iredell County begins.

This is dairy country. Iredell produces more milk than any other county in the state and calls itself "Dairyland of the Southeastern United States." But the county also claims to produce more baby chicks than any other place on earth. These facts explain all the dairy barns and chicken houses by the roadside.

At the bottom of the dollar sign, the highway reaches Statesville, the county seat, a town that bears a name held by no other community in the country. How that name came about, however, is lost to history. It may have been because the people of the original settlement, first called Fourth Creek Community, wanted to honor the original 13 states, or simple because the settlement was a popular stopover on the once-famous States Road.

The highway passes through the center of Statesville, entering from the east along Davie Street, elegant with its big trees and old two-story houses, through downtown past the distinctive red-brick city hall, proclaimed to be the finest example of Richardsonian Romanesque architecture in the state, out of town to the west along West Front Street, where travelers looking for a place to sleep can find the Snow White and Seven Rooms Tourist Home. Now 64 has joined with U.S. 70 for a 50-mile run to Morganton.

On the western edge of Statesville, the Friendly Family Restaurant includes a thought for today on its menu: "What I am to be I am now becoming." Not far away, as the highway leaves town, the Winecoff Marble and Granite Works, a grave marker company, provides another thought. "Drive Slow," says a thin marker standing in front of rows of display markers. "We Can Wait."

The hills become more pronounced as the highway makes its way westward toward Catawba County. Some bear red scars where bulldozers have slashed parking spots for new mobile homes.

Abandoned truck-weighing stations on both sides of the road at one point testify to the highway's loss of stature, but one of the stations, on the south side, has been transformed into a tiny, neat home dwarfed with driveway.

Kudzu monsters hulk on the banks of the Catawba River as the highway passes by bridge into Catawba County. A few miles later, a roadside park by a small stream beckons. The traveler willing to hike a few hundred yards along the stream can cross Bunker Hill Covered Bridge, built in 1894, high over Lyles Creek, a favored spot for lovers who come to leave their names entwined on the bridge's huge timbers.

A cemetery offers greeting to Claremont, a town crowded by factory traffic at midafternoon. Industrial plants line the highway to Conover, the only town in the state named for an Italian sculptor, Canova, whose statue of George Washington was lost in the fire that destroyed the state capitol in 1831.

At Conover, the highway changes to four lanes again, joined now with U.S. 321 for a brief stretch. On a ridge west of town, a faint blue image comes on the horizon. Mountains. Not just hills with memories of past glories. Real mountains lie ahead.

The Demands of Horses

COOL SPRINGS   Midday, and the horses in the big red barn at Quarter Boot Farm are at ease, cooling in their stalls. Lynn Isenhour should be so lucky.

He is red-faced and sweating profusely as he forks wood shavings so the horses may sleep more comfortably. The simultaneous arrival of a frosty soft drink fetched by a co-worker and a visitor wanting to talk offers a welcome break. He walks to the tack room on the other side of the barn, flops into a chair amid the saddles, props his booted feet on the edge of a desk and takes a big gulp of his drink. A thermometer by the door registers 90.

"Weather like this," he says, taking off his hat and fanning himself with it, "horses, you can't work 'em in the middle of the day. They can't take that. They get heatstroke. They're just like humans."

Horses demand a lot of people who love them, and after giving up two marriages and a job because of them, Lynn, at age 32, is beginning to accept that. Now he is able to give them his undivided attention, and even that sometimes is not enough.

He jokes about working 18-hour days and eight-day weeks, but it isn't much of an exaggeration. Weekdays, he usually is in the saddle by 6 in the morning, training until 10, at chores during the middle of the day while the horses rest, back in the saddle again about 4 for another four hours of riding, and before bedtime there's usually book work. Weekends, he's on the road in his double-cab truck pulling a long, enclosed trailer heavy with horses, going to horse shows.

"I guess when it's in your blood," he says, "you just have to do it."

Probably a pony named Dan put it in his blood. His daddy gave him that pony when he was 6, and he has fond memories of riding it around the family dairy farm in the East Mombo community, now under the waters of Lake Norman.

Later, his daddy got him a quarter horse named Sir Go Dan, and he trained it as a 4-H club project.

"I started to train horses for other people when I was 15," he says.

But he saw horses only as an avocation, and after high school he went to technical college to study transportation, thinking it might get him a good job with a trucking company. Instead, he got married, went to work for the telephone company, bought some land, built himself a barn and riding ring and went on training horses.

"I'd come home from the phone company and ride till 11 or 12 or 1 o'clock at night," he says. "Friday came and I'd leave out and go to horse shows all weekend."

123

He lost his farm in the divorce settlement, and for a while he went to horse shows with nothing to show. It was more than he could stand. So six years ago he found this barn, abandoned, dilapidated, hulking on the South Yadkin River.

"This was an old milk barn," he says, "Really, the biggest still in North Carolina was found right here."

Actually, the still was in a chicken house just up the hill. Underground pipes led from the still to the barn where the liquor was stored in milk tanks.

"Milk tanker would come down here and instead of hauling milk, they were hauling likker," Lynn says. "I trained horses for the guy that owned the still. He told me one time, he said. 'You'll never make as much money off of this place as I made off of it.'"

Love of horses, not money, was driving Lynn as he cleared land, built stalls, holding pens, a riding ring, refurbished the barn and painted it red, landscaped the grounds, and as a final touch decorated the barn with petunias and geraniums. He did it all after work and on weekends when there were no horse shows to attend—and got married again in the meantime.

Two years ago, the telephone company wanted to change his work schedule, making it almost impossible for him to attend horse shows anymore, so he quit his job.

"I had to make a decision, and I haven't regretted it yet," he says.

Since then, he has devoted most of his energies to boarding, training, breeding and showing horses.

"This is basically a training and breeding barn," he says. "I like the breeding business. During breeding season, that's the hardest time. This season we bred close to 100 mares down here. You breed from January to June to get an early baby. You want a mare to foal from February to May. You don't want mares to have babies in hot summer. Lots of flies. It's hard on 'em."

Most of the horses he boards, trains and shows are studs. One, a 6-year-old gray quarter horse named Trouble's Tribute, in which Lynn owns a quarter share, is a champion that commands a $750 stud fee and has been bred to as many as five mares in a day.

"That horse is worth a hundred thousand dollars," Lynn says. "His daddy was high point halter horse in the nation. A halter horse, that's something like a beauty pageant. That's judged on a horse's conformation, his build, head, neck, muscles, how he's put together. They're judged on the way they look, how they travel, how well-balanced they are."

He goes to the stall and brings Trouble's Tribute out to show him off in the riding ring, then takes him back and returns to forking shavings.

"This business, it's so hectic, you've got to have a love for it," he says. "I couldn't ask for it to be any better. I'm content, happy, getting the bills paid and doing what I want to do."

The Last Cotton Gin

COOL SPRINGS   Bristol Robertson rousts himself from the sofa where he has been napping and calls to his wife, Hazel.

"Where's my shoes?" he says. "Give me some chewin' tobaccer. A man can't gin cotton without chewin' tobaccer."

Ginning cotton is something that Bristol, usually called B.C., does now only in memory. He is 80, and two heart attacks and the wears of time have taken their toll.

"Yessir," he says, "I ginned the last bale of cotton in Iredell County. I sure did."

Twelve years ago, that was. B.C. cranked up the massive machinery at Cool Springs Ginning Co. to gin a single bale.

Cotton had been a long time going in Iredell County. Once it was the major crop.

"It was solid both sides of the road from here to Statesville and from here to Mocksville," B.C. says. "Both sides of the road."

That was why he chose Cool Springs for the site of his gin in the first place. In the early '20s, he had started another gin with his father in the Charles community about 14 miles south.

"We bought a second-handed outfit. I paid for it with my sawmilling money. It was just a small, one-horse outfit. When we started ginning up there we did 600 bales a year. It was too small a business for me and my daddy both. We got married and I started looking for a place to make a living. I wanted a bigger territory and a bigger place so I got out roving around huntin' a location, me and my daddy together. I measured the distance from here to Statesville and from here to Mocksville and between here and where I lived at and I decided this was it."

He bought two acres of land on the side of State Road 90, soon to become U.S. 64. There he put up a building of big timbers and corrugated metal and moved another second-hand gin into it in 1930.

"I ginned 700 bales the first year, and I ginned 1,400 the second year and I ginned 1,800 the third year. Went on to 2,200 bales. Then it turned around on me in 19 and. . . ." He takes a long pause, trying to remember. "It turned around on me in 19 and 40. It just drifted on down to nothing. In the 1930s, the only income they had around here was what I give 'em. Take a depression to put cotton back in this county."

The gin was more than a source of income for area farmers. From October through December, the ginning time, it was a scene of great activity, a focal point, a community gathering place.

"It was a lot of fun around a cotton gin,'" says B.C.'s son, Bill, who grew up around the gin and lives next door to it. "Lots of stories exchanged, lot of laughing and going on. Dad used to keep apples in the office for the farmers and the kids. Every year after all the farmers had gathered their crops, they'd have a big rabbit barbecue down here."

Cotton hit its highest price ever during World War II, and the gin was going strong. But on a blustery October night in 1944, lightning struck the gin and it burned to the ground. More than 125 bales of cotton burned with it, many of them owned by farmers. B.C. had no insurance, but he paid the farmers for every bale they lost, then used his lifetime savings to rebuild the gin, this time of concrete blocks and steel. He filled it with new equipment, including four 80-saw gins, at a cost of $75,000, a large sum for the time.

The '50s brought a decline in cotton, and B.C. bought land and began growing it himself. He invested in three automatic cotton pickers and used them to pick other farmers' cotton as well as his own. Nothing seemed to be able to stem the decline, and by the mid-'60s, B.C. knew it was hopeless.

"Beetles got pretty bad in this territory, and it got so cheap. Seemed like even the growing season changed on us. Didn't nobody want to grow cotton anymore. Ginned 12 bales the year before I quit. Ginned one bale the last year. Some of the farmers begged me to leave the gin so it could be operated. I just kept it because they asked me to, and I thought cotton might just come back sometime, but it ain't going to come back. I'd like to have a sale for it now."

Now B.C. is about to do something he doesn't like to do anymore. In his house, next door to his son's, he puts on his shoes and checkered hat, gets his walking stick and chewing tobacco and climbs into a car for the short ride to the gin.

"It makes me feel bad to look at it," he says. "To think what I have done and go out there and see a dead something."

The ginning company buildings sit surrounded by weeds and undergrowth, used now only as shelter for his son's farming equipment. Vines twine through broken windows. Mud daubers and spiders have decorated the rusting machinery inside.

B.C. walks slowly through the dark building, pointing with his walking stick, describing every step of the ginning process.

"Get all of this junk out of here and I could get this thing a'goin' again in a day," he says.

His son, who is principal at a nearby school and part-time farmer, has been working in a nearby field. He parks his tractor in the spot where wagons and trucks used to stop to have their loads of cotton sucked into the gin, and comes inside to join the conversation.

"I got a lifetime tied up in this thing," B.C. says. "I put the thing up for that boy right there. I figured he'd run it someday. Man spend $75,000 to put his son in business and then him just walk away and leave it."

Bill, who is 50, has heard this before. He operated the gin one season after college, then went back to get a master's degree. He laughs.

"But daddy," he says, "there wasn't any cotton."

The physical strain of touring the plant has been too great for B.C. He has to be helped into the car, then helped back into his house, his steps slow and faltering.

"I'm actually not sick," he says. "In a way I'm just wore out. But, dear Lord, I've been a man in my lifetime."

Horseshoe Pitchers' Mecca

STATESVILLE   "This is it," Jack Springer says with obvious pride. "We've got one of the largest horseshoe pitching facilities in the world. There's none bigger than ours in the United States, and only a few as big. Winston-Salem used to be the horseshoe king bee of North Carolina. Now we are. There's no question about that."

Credit Jack for that. The city does.

"Now at the world's tournament in 1983, they had a big ceremony and named these courts after me," he says. "They're going to put a brick thing up with a plaque on it with my name—I've already seen the plaque—but they just haven't got around to it yet."

Jack brims with enthusiasm when he talks about horseshoes. It was that enthusiasm that turned Statesville into a horseshoe pitching center, caused the city to build 24 lighted horseshoe courts in Lakewood Park, and brought two world tournaments and several annual statewide and national tournaments to the town.

Yet, Jack knew very little about horseshoes when he set all this in motion in 1969. The town was about to have its first Dogwood Festival, and Jack was a member of a committee planning it.

"We were just sitting there trying to figure out what events to have," he remembers. "I just mentioned, 'Let's have a horseshoe tournament.' Somebody said, 'That's a good idea.'"

Jack had organized horseshoe tournaments before when he was athletics officer at Camp Lee, Va., during World War II, but other sports attracted most of his attention them. His unbeaten boxing team included light heavyweight champion Billy Conn, who twice fought Joe Louis for the heavyweight championship. World champion Danno O'Mahoney was star of his wrestling team. Tony Ruffa, who kicked the winning field goal in the Rose Bowl when it was held in Durham, was captain of his football team. His track team included Olympic runner Barney Ewell. Several college stars played on his championship basketball team.

With all that to claim his attention, Jack just didn't get very worked up about horseshoes then.

Neither did he have anything to do with horseshoes when he became commandant and coach at Fishburne Military School, from which he had graduated, in Waynesboro, Va.; nor during the years he was a high school coach in Virginia.

In 1954, Jack's next-door neighbor, who happened to be from Statesville, told him that the town was looking for a recreation director. Jack applied and got the job that would lead him to become

Jack Springer

one of North Carolina's biggest promoters of horseshoes.

For that first tournament at the Dogwood Festival, Jack got the city to build 12 courts and got some noted area pitchers—J.D. Goforth, Gurney York and Guy Jones—to help him organize it. He sent notices to horseshoe pitching groups and got a much bigger turnout than he'd anticipated. By the second year, he was getting participants from several states, and by the third year he'd gotten the city to build six more courts.

So popular was the spring tournament that Jack started a fall tournament as well. More and more pitchers came from a wider and wider area, including some who were officials of the National Horseshoe Pitcher's Association.

"At one tournament, some guy said, 'Jack, you know, if you could ever get 24 courts here, you could have the world's tournament.'"

Jack needed no more encouragement. He got the city to build six more courts, light them and install bleachers for spectators, and then make a bid. So it was that in 1977 Statesville had the world tournament for the first time.

Ironically, Jack fell ill a few weeks before the tournament and got to attend only on an ambulance stretcher, wheeled in long enough to see a few pitches and pose for a picture with Gov. Jim Hunt.

He was fit by the time Statesville got its second world tournament in 1983 and devoted himself to seeing that it came off successfully. By then he was retired after working 28 years for the city, and had become an energetic, unpaid promoter of horseshoe pitching.

"Horseshoe courts are springing up all over," he says. "It's amazing how many are being built. Interest is really growing. It's a great sport. And it's good exercise. There was an article in a medical magazine this doctor wrote where he rated horseshoes way above bowling because of the walking and the bending over and the throwing. You're throwing two and a half pounds, you know."

Beyond his fondness for the sport, Jack had just come to like horseshoe pitchers.

"The nicest people you can ever run into are horseshoe pitchers," he says. "They don't argue. They're good sports and what I call . . . well, they're good Americans. They're working people. They're the kind of people who make this country what it is."

Jack is now secretary-treasurer of the N.C. Horseshoe Pitchers Association. As director of the youth committee for the national association he is looking for ways to get more young people into the sport. He spends a lot of time planning, promoting and organizing tournaments.

He's also an officer in the Shriners, president of his Sunday school class, a director of the Dogwood Festival, and at 67, leads three one-hour exercise classes—calisthenics, aerobics, running, stretching, dancing—three days a week and walks two miles every night with a neighborhood group.

One thing he doesn't do, and never has, is pitch horseshoes.

"I'm just not a horseshoe pitcher," he says. "Sometimes I think I'd like to get out and pitch but, you know, I just don't have time."

The Snowball Man

CLAREMONT   It looks like a carnival encampment by the side of the highway on the eastern edge of town. A collection of old buses. A few other broken-down vehicles. A line of gaily painted vans. A candy apple and cotton candy stand on a trailer.

No carnival. Just home and business headquarters for Lucky Tony Millsaps, the snowball man.

Tony is 42, tall, goateed, with thinning reddish hair, father of nine, former race driver and hippie, a snowball entrepreneur since childhood.

"Whenever I was 7 years old, I had a little stand on my back porch in Kannapolis," he says. "I sold snow cones for three cents. Had a big old ice box on the porch and I'd scrape 'em by hand. We lived on 16th Street, about a block from the ice plant. I used to take my wagon up there and get a quarter block of ice, which was about all I could pull. It was a way to make money to go to the movies on Saturday. It made me feel like I was somebody."

A few years later, Tony's dad, Dick, fixed a snowball box on the back of an old car and went into the snowball business himself. Tony helped him for a while.

"Then whenever I was 15, I'd saved up a couple of hundred dollars and I bought me a '41 Studebaker for $40. My uncle, he helped me fix a box on the back of it, and I paid my cousin who had a driver's license $2 a day to drive for me."

Since then he's been on the streets selling snowballs every year but one. That year, when he was 22, he spent in prison for stealing hubcaps, although he says it was friends who did the stealing; he just got caught with them.

In a bus where he keeps his ice machine and cotton candy equipment, Tony sits, shirtless and sweating, thumbing through photo albums, showing off pictures of snowball rigs he built and cars he raced. There's the old three-wheeled scooter he sold snowballs from when he first got out of prison. And there it is painted red, white and blue for the Bicentennial celebration. There, too, is the old Merita Bread truck he bought in '72 after he got married for the third time.

"Still had the forms in it you could sign up for the Lone Ranger Club," he says. "That was my first truck."

He was married the first time at 16. That marriage gave him two children. He had one child by his second marriage, which lasted two years. His third marriage brought two more. After that, he gave

131

Lucky Tony Millsaps

up on marriage but not on children. He had three by a girlfriend and one by an acquaintance.

He now lives with a much younger woman who has one child, not his, and he is through having children to add to his list of support payments.

"As soon as we started goin' together," he says, "I went and spent $1,000 on her to have her tubes tied."

Racing was another passion for Tony. He built his first race car from junkyard parts in 1963. He built another after he got out of prison and started racing in the rookie division at Hickory Speedway.

"That's the one I won my first race in right there," he says, showing a snapshot of a car. "And that was the end of it right there," he says of a shot of a wrecked car. "Hit the wall."

He was track champion in his division in 1969 but gave up racing the following year because he couldn't afford the equipment to advance.

"Quit racing and started partying," he says. "Became a hippie and started smoking pot."

By the mid-'70s, Tony had changed from hippie to capitalist. He had two trucks and a scooter on the streets selling snowballs, cotton candy, candy apples; and in 1975 he bought a trailer stand for cotton candy and snowballs and started working the State Fair. In 1976 he used money he and his wife had made painting apartments to buy four surplus used mail vans, which he painted in bright colors and put on the road.

He was living in Statesville then, and kids in the neighborhoods he worked called him Lucky because some of his snowball cups had lucky marks in them good for a free snowball. He called his company the Lucky Cup Snowball Co. but he painted "The Candy Van" on his trucks because he liked the sound of it.

At one time he envisioned fleets of Candy Van trucks all over America. "I had goals of expanding up like McDonald's or Hardee's or something in every town. But now I've seen all the book work and regulations and stuff, and it would just be a headache."

In 1980, he took his vans, his snowball trailer and a few other things and set up camp in this field by a creek. He bought an old bus and outfitted it with a water bed, a wood stove, appliances, a shower and moved into it. The encampment has grown piecemeal since, and now includes another well-appointed bus where his 10-year-old son lives.

"I moved up here to get away from my ex-girlfriend in Statesville," he says. "Me and her didn't get along too good, so I just moved out here. Last year she even come out here raisin' hell, throwin' things. We had it pretty rough last summer. But we're friendly now. She drives one of my trucks on weekends."

Tony goes out in one of his trucks every day but Wednesday, as does his current girlfriend. Sometimes he hires part-time help to take other trucks out, but they usually don't last long.

"It requires a certain type person to sell snowballs," he says. "Not just anybody can do it. They's a lot more to it than just handing out a snowball. It's a complicated job. You got to be a person that's got a good personality. You got to be able to talk about fishing if the customer wants to talk about fishing. You got to be able to talk about tennis, golf, whatever the customer wants to talk about. You got to get along good with small children. You got to have a lot of patience and basically you got to be a good-hearted, friendly person. It's strenuous work. It's hot. Sometimes you got 10 or 15 kids all hollering at the same time. They want this and they want that. You make one thing and they want something else. Some of these people go out and they come in and say they just can't do it."

Mostly it is late afternoon and early-evening work but it is sporadic, greatly affected by the timing of pay checks and weather. This summer has not been good.

"We've been having a lot of rainy weather," Tony says. "We haven't got in but about one full day in a week and a half. Sometimes we do all right. We have times when we make a couple of hundred dollars a day and then we have weeks when we don't make a penny. We always do good at the State Fair. Hadn't been for the State Fair we'd'a starved to death last winter, I reckon.

"Usually, in the summertime, we eat pretty good and buy a few clothes. In the wintertime is when we have it hard. In the wintertime it's kinda lean livin'. Kinda like an ol' wolf in the Rockies. Live rough in the wintertime."

Despite that, Tony can't envision himself doing anything else.

"I'm in it till the day I die, I guess," he says. "There's something about sellin' snowballs. Just like now, I can go out there and sell snow cones and everybody comes up and is so nice and friendly, and you sell 'em a snowball and make 'em happy and it makes you feel good. If you don't go out there, it's almost like you lettin' 'em down. It gives you a feeling of accomplishment. It's like it was when I was little. It makes you feel like you *are* somebody."

A Yearning to Race

HICKORY   At 6:30, an hour and a half before race time, a crisis arose.

The NASCAR man found fault with the tires. The left side tires were slightly bigger than the right side, and that would not do. If he wanted to race, the NASCAR man told Tim Canipe, all four tires had to be the same.

That dejected Tim. These were the only tires he had. It made his wife, Paulette, nearly furious.

"They just give him a hard time anyway," she said.

Half an hour later, the problem was solved. Tim checked the spare tire in his Pinto, the car he'd driven to the track, and found it was the same size as the left side tires on his racer. Then he found a friend who also drove a Pinto and borrowed his spare. It took him and his brother, Ronnie, only a few minutes to get the tires on the car, but Tim wasn't greatly encouraged.

"They'll probably find something else," he said.

This was a big night at Hickory Speedway—a ⅜-mile paved track at the side of U.S. 64 built as a dirt track in the early '50s, now one of the oldest stock-car tracks in the country—and Tim really wanted to race and look good doing it. The crowd was bigger than usual, several thousand people, drawn by special events.

In addition to the regular Saturday-night races in the limited, late model, mini and bomber divisions, NASCAR's sleek Darlington Dash cars had come for a special 100-lap race; and one of stock-car racing's greatest heroes, Junior Johnson, was present as grand marshall.

Tim's car, a '72 Opel, was parked in the infield between the first and second turns. It was entered in the ministock division. These are the smallest and cheapest stock-car racers. In the ministock division anybody with a yearning to race can put a few hundred dollars into an old junk car and get on the track.

A yearning to race was something that Tim believed had been born in him. He'd practically grown up at Hickory Speedway. His daddy, Glen, a truck driver, had raced here until his car hit the corner of the first turn wall head-on one night about 10 years ago and left him in the hospital for three months. His older brother, Dexter, is one of the top drivers at the track in the top division, late model. His three other brothers have served as mechanics and crewmen. His uncle, J.V. Huffman, owns two of the best cars that race at the

135

Tim Canipe with his car

track in the limited and late-model divisions. His 16-year-old cousin, Robert Huffman, is one of the track's rising stars in the limited division.

In the last five years, Tim and his wife have missed only one race at the track, and all that time he was yearning to race. He had raced part of one season, when he was 16, in an ancient Olds 98 that he and his brothers patched together, but that ended when he wrecked it beyond hope. Money had kept him from racing since then.

He had married three years earlier at 18. He and Paulette bought a trailer and parked it behind his daddy's house. A year later, Paulette had a baby, Tim Jr., called T.J. Tim had a good job as a mechanic at a cotton mill, but it took all he made just to get along. There just wasn't money for racing.

But finally the yearning had overcome him. Two and a half weeks ago, Tim had done some trading with a fellow at a junkyard and came home pulling the little Opel. He and Ronnie tore into it. They ripped out the seats, built a roll-cage, took out windows, welded doors shut, started tinkering with the engine. They worked on it every night until nearly midnight, hardly taking time to eat.

In a week and a half they'd finished. Tim had painted the car two shades of blue. On the doors he painted big 75s, the number his uncle used on his more professional racers. On the fenders and top he painted the names of service stations and garages that had given him discounts on parts and supplies, and over the door, he painted, "Tim." He had about $125 in the car.

A week earlier, he brought the car to the track for its first trial, started last and had to quit after only two laps when the engine started missing. Four days later, after hours of tinkering with the engine, he was back at the track for practice. Paulette and T.J. came with him.

As much as Paulette loves racing, she admitted that Wednesday afternoon that she has a different perspective of it when Tim is on the track. Then it makes her nervous.

"I want him to do it," she said, "because he wants to do it, but if it was up to me and he'd listen to what I said, I'd say no."

On the track, Tim was demonstrating why she felt that way. He was going hard, nearly losing control every time he went into the first turn, never backing off.

Paulette watched anxiously from the back of Ronnie's pickup truck, clutching her son.

"Daddy's goina wreck," she kept saying to the baby. "Yeah, daddy's goina wreck. He's goina wreck it good, T.J."

He almost did. On his last lap, he lost control, spun wildly and came to a stop against the wall of the back straightaway. A bigger, faster car spun trying to avoid him and nearly hit him broadside.

"Oh no, whoa!" Paulette yelled as the other car spun toward Tim. "Your daddy wrecked! Your daddy wrecked!"

After she calmed and Tim returned unflustered to the pits ("I know he seen me," was his only comment about the incident), Paulette tried to explain why her husband races.

"He's one of these people that he loves the thrill of it. He's wild or something. He's just one of these people that, well . . . Fast. That's the word. Down the interstate or down the track, he's going fast. That ain't no lie. I have my seat belt on everywhere I go with him."

Now Tim was ready to race. Nobody had come to recheck his tires. But at 7:30 when the loudspeakers called all drivers to the garage for a meeting, he went and hunkered in a corner on bags of material used for drying oil spills on the track.

A track official started calling roll, minidivision first. "Seventy-five," he said, first number.

Tim didn't answer until somebody nudged him. "About to forget my damn number," he muttered.

Tim wanted to know only two things from the meeting: when his race would be run and what his starting position would be. His first question was answered soon after roll call. The limited race would be first, followed by the Darlington cars, the late models, then the ministocks and bombers for just 15 laps each. The meeting ended with no mention of the lineup for the 23 minicars, and Tim made his way through the crowd to a track official to see what he could find out.

He emerged from the crowd elated. The lineup would be the same as the roll call. He would start first, and nobody had said a word about his tires. He hurried to the pits and found Paulette sitting in the cab of Ronnie's truck. She looked at him expectantly.

"Couldn't be no better," he said.

"What?" she said.

"Right on the pole."

"No! You're fulla . . ."

He grinned. "Right on the pole."

Tim worked in the pits for his cousin during the first race, which his cousin won, leading all the way. For the next race he perched with relatives on wide, smooth racing tires in a rack over the cab of his uncle's truck, parked by the rail at the first turn. Normally, he would have been in the pits helping his brother, Dexter, during the late-model race, but Dexter had engine problems and had gone to the beach. So Tim remained on the truck until that race got down to the last 10 laps. Then he hopped down and went over to his little Opel.

Most other drivers wore fancy driving uniforms with lots of patches, but Tim slid through the driver's window in his blue jeans, strapped on an old blue helmet and sat revving his engine.

After Wednesday's practice, he and Ronnie had worked two more nights on the engine. He even bought some new parts, but he wouldn't tell Paulette how much they cost.

She stood by the car talking to him as the late-model race finished. As soon at it was over, Tim spun onto the track in a dust cloud.

"He's nervous," Paulette said, "because he's up front, and he don't know how the car's goina do."

In calling out the lineup, the track announcer called Tim by the wrong name, Walker, which made Paulette mad. She climbed onto a stand reserved for rescue squad members to watch the race. Tim's brother and other relatives clambered onto his uncle's truck, and Tim grinned at them as the pace car led the cars slowly into the first turn.

"Hope there ain't no cautions," Ronnie said. "He might win it. All the fast cars are in the back."

After two laps the pace car darted into the pits and the flagman waved green. Tim's Opel suddenly disappeared into the pack. Six, seven, eight cars shot across the starting line ahead of him.

"Done started missing," said Ronnie, jumping off the truck, shaking his head.

Tim whipped into the infield angry and embarrassed. "Lost all the damn power," he shouted. "I mashed the gas, and it was like that thing went in reverse." Ronnie was already under the hood, pulling out spark plugs.

The flagman had signaled a restart, and the cars began lining up again. Tim made it back onto the track for the pace laps, last now instead of first. He ran two laps after the start, falling steadily back from the pack, then pulled back into the infield when a spinning car brought a yellow flag.

Ronnie and a couple of helpers were once again under the hood. Tim shouted instructions out the window. The race began again. Tim could see the laps ticking down on the scoreboard. Finally, he took off his helmet in disgust and climbed out of the car.

As the winner was claiming his trophy and $75 prize from the speedway queen at the start-finish line, Tim was tearing into his carburetor. He struck a match to see and announced he'd found the problem.

"Damn screw came out of the carburetor. I bet they ain't another screw like that in 20 miles."

He had started first, finished last. His winnings were $5. But at least he was racing.

"Just try again next week," he said. "This week, I'll go a little deeper in that motor. Jerk the damn head off this week."

Ghost Winery

ICARD   Half the big door has been battered and ripped away, leaving the cellar open to the hot air.

"I didn't even know this door was knocked down," Mellie Jean Bernard says, stepping gingerly inside. The floor is covered with mud, washed in by the rains.

"This is really a swamp in here. Watch yourself. It's slick. You can tell it's just like air conditioning in here. Just the right temperature. Those redwood vats, they've never had a thing done to them since we closed the winery, and they're just as good as they ever were."

There are 110 of the huge vats, shipped from California and installed in 1933, each capable of holding 1,000 gallons of wine. But the last wine was taken from them in 1948, pumped into railroad cars and hauled north as vinegar, sold at 15 cents a gallon, a heavy loss for Mellie Jean's father.

Forced to close by legislation, Bernard's Waldensian Wines, North Carolina bonded winery No. 7, became a ghostly presence on the side of U.S. Highway 64. Until three years ago, when a mysterious fire destroyed the offices and damaged the warehouse over the cellar, the winery remained unchanged from the day Mellie Jean's father locked the doors in 1948. Now Mellie Jean is trying to put some of his father's old equipment back to use again.

His father was born in Sicily, a hunter's son. He worked his way to this country as a cabin boy on an ocean liner in 1906 when he was 16. In 1917 he heard the government was going to build dams at Muscle Shoals, Ala., applied for a job on the project and was turned down. So he changed his name from Carmello D. Bernardo to Mellie D. Bernard, reapplied and was hired immediately.

From the Muscle Shoals project, Mellie D. was sent to help build Bridgewater Dam to hold back Lake James in western Burke County. While there, he started courting Rose Giles, who lived in nearby Glen Alpine. When he was sent to work on the Badin Dam in Stanly County, he bought a Model T Ford and drove it back and forth to Burke County to see Rose. After they married, he hooked up with a mechanic and started a garage in Icard in eastern Burke County, and there he and Rose settled and started a family.

The garage grew into a service station and store. By the early '30s, Mellie had an oil distributorship and a chain of 11 service stations.

One day in 1933, a fellow from Virginia came to see him, a government man. He was looking for a partner with money to start

Mellie J. Bernard in bottling room where he once worked

a winery. Prohibition was about to end, he said, and a lot of money could be made. This area on the edge of the mountains would be a good spot for a winery because it had a lot of fruit.

"My daddy didn't know anything about wine," Mellie Jean says, "except what he'd learned in the old country, you know, as a boy, helping make it. They made a lot of it, but it was crude. They kept it on the table and drank it every meal. He said they poured it at the table the same as milk."

Mellie D. was taken with the idea nonetheless, and after the fellow from Virginia backed out, he went ahead with the plan.

"I helped build the winery," Mellie Jean says. "I helped haul the rock in for the foundation and all. Helped make the wine, helped bottle it. I was the bottler. Drove a truck and distributed it. I was in it from the building of the building until it was completely closed."

Mellie D. sold his first wine in 1935. The name for it, Bernard's Waldensian, was suggested by a friend in the oil business, the brother of Georgia Gov. Eugene Talmadge, because Mellie D. got some of his recipes from Waldensian immigrants from northern Italy in the nearby town of Valdese. The same friend designed the label, which originally showed a man in a tuxedo and a woman in an evening gown saluting each other with wine glasses. The government denied that lable on the grounds that it was immoral for a woman to be shown with a wine glass, so it was redone to have her holding a rose.

The wine was a success from the beginning.

"It was no problem to sell all the wine we could make," Mellie Jean says. "They would come from everywhere to get it. We sold about 60,000 gallons a year."

The biggest seller turned out to be scuppernong, but it was a while before that came along, because Mellie D. aged it eight years. But he made plenty of younger wines with other grapes, James, Concord, Catawba, Niagara. And other fruits, too. Blackberries, apples, peaches, apricots.

"We bought our fruit from local farmers," Mellie Jean says. "I remember we advertised in the paper and on the radio, 14 cents a gallon for blackberries. Farmers that had large families would bring in 50, 60, sometimes as many as a hundred gallons of blackberries. Later we went up to 18 cents, and I remember paying 21 cents a gallon. It really helped the farmers out. You take a farmer with 10 kids, bring in 30 gallons of blackberries, he could buy quite a bit of groceries back then."

Another big seller was pokeberry.

"We had heard that pokeberry wine was good for rheumatism," Mellie J. says. "We started making it and sold it as fast as we could make it. People swore it helped their rheumatism."

The wines were distributed throughout western North Carolina and shipped by special order to other areas and even to some other countries. The winery was the only spot in Burke County where alcoholic beverages could be sold legally and that prompted opposition. Eventually, the opponents were able to get a law through the legislature banning the manufacture of wine in Burke County. Mellie D. had 60,000 gallons on hand and a month to get rid of it.

After the winery closed, Mellie D. remained in oil and real estate until he sold out and retired. He died in 1980 at age 90. Mellie Jean worked with his father until 1952 when he got rights to distribute Cadillacs in Morganton and started his own business. He sold his dealership in 1982 and has since built a skating rink.

The old winery, which he inherited, stayed on Mellie Jean's mind. He wanted to revive his daddy's wines, and in 1983 he entered a partnership to do just that. He joined with Lorin Weaver, who owns Kathryn's Cheese House, a delicatessen, gourmet food, wine and gift shop on U.S. 64 west of Hickory in Catawba County, and Leonard Bumgarner, a professional beekeeper noted for his sourwood honey. They bought into a winery in Duplin County, which this year began turning out wines under the Bernards' Waldensian label, all grape wines, four whites, three reds, and soon scuppernong champagne.

Mellie Jean and his partners also moved some of the equipment from the old winery last fall and set up Bernard's Waldensian Winery Museum in one end of Kathryn's Cheese House, from which they are selling the wine. Their hope is to someday begin making some of the old-time fruit wines at the site, blackberry, peach, apple. They will add sourwood honey wine, mead, to the list, as well, although that will probably be a while.

"Mead, the older it gets the better it gets," says Leonard, who already has a batch working. "It gets to the point it will bubble like champagne. When you open mead, if it's aged properly, it will just roll bubbles up in your glass. I expect we'll age it at least four years. It'll be expensive, I know that. This sourwood honey brings five bucks a pound. When you start using that stuff to make wine, it's probably going to be $15 or more a bottle."

Whether he'll ever be able to put all the old winery equipment back to use again, Mellie Jean is uncertain. He shines a flashlight over the big vats in the cool dark cellar as he explains how the wine used to be made.

"Look at the caps," he says, entering the bottling room, which was shut down with bottles on line waiting to be filled. "There's some bottles never got used. Here's our original old bottling machine. I sat here like this, put two here and two there, a one-man bottling operation."

Later, he steps out of the dark coolness of the cellar back into the sunlight, wiping mud from his shoes.

"Lots of old memories in there," he says. "I've got to get this door fixed."

The Fish That Love Sugar Pops

ICARD   The lake covers 10 acres by the side of the highway. For more than 40 years, it was a private fishing pond, stocked with bass and bluegill, crappie and blue channel catfish.

For several years, Bob Bernard, who inherited the lake from his father, operated a pawn shop beside it and let people fish for a dollar or two. But the lake wasn't bringing in enough to pay taxes on it, and the pawn shop wasn't doing all that well either. So this summer, Bob changed things.

Now the lake is an attraction, lined with shelters, strung with lights, beseeching attention with big signs—and attracting lots of people with strange concoctions and visions of easy money in their heads.

The old attraction is as old and as simple as gambling. Lake Bernard has become Bernard's Prize Carp Lake. The carp are prized for the money they can bring.

This is how it works.

Sunday through Thursday, the lake is open from 7:30 a.m. to 9 p.m. Anybody who wants to fish can pay $3 for a day's privilege. Anybody who pays can then enter jackpots. Fifty cents buys a chance in the hourly jackpot. The person who catches the biggest carp that hour claims all the money. Entry into the daily pot costs $3.75. Those catching the three biggest fish of the day claim that pot. A quarter can claim the daily pot for the smallest fish. For 50 cents a day, a person can get into the 20-pound pot, which builds daily until somebody catches a fish weighing 20 pounds or more. This pot frequently climbs above $100.

The same rules hold on Friday and Saturday from 7:30 a.m. to 6 p.m. But at 7 p.m. on those days, the serious fishing begins. Each person fishing must pay $18.75. Every hour until 3 a.m. $40 is given away, $25 for the biggest fish, $15 for next biggest. At 3 a.m., prizes are given for the four-largest and the smallest fish caught that night, calculated according to the number of participants. The best night for a single entrant so far has been $181.

"These boys are fanatics about this fishing," Bob says, settling into an old metal glider at lakeside. "They just stay with it and a lot of 'em make money with it. They really do. It kinda gets in their blood like playing blackjack or poker. They just get hooked on it. It's where the money is in fishing now."

Bob decided to change to a prize lake after visiting a few others that were operating successfully in western North Carolina.

"They're getting popular all over," he says.

Late this spring, he stocked 42,000 pounds of carp, ranging in size from seven to 25 pounds, trucked in from Lake Erie at a cost of 38 cents a pound. Fishermen are required to release all carp they catch, but still he'll be restocking this fall with even larger fish.

"We lose some," he says. "We're losing about 350 pounds a week, I figure. They get hooked too deep and so forth. And some fishermen, they'll use baits that kill 'em. We have two things we ban. Horse feed. The fish hit it real good. But it has a medication in it that kills worms in horses. It'll also kill your fish. And no uncooked corn. A carp will eat a whole bunch of it and when it gets in his belly it swells and swells and it bursts his stomach, kills the fish.

"We check baits every hour. We look in every bucket. You've got to do it. If you don't they'll kill all your fish. These guys, they're fishing for money, they'll fish with anything. They'll use battery acid on their bait, which draws fish to it, I don't know why. They'll use strychnine, which is deadly poison, but something about it draws the fish. We have to be real careful, and we've had to make a rule, if the fish when it's weighed and put back in the water don't swim away, it don't count.

"I think the most fantastic thing about this fishing is the baits they use. You really wouldn't believe what all they use to catch carp with. A carp, you know, is vegetarian. He'll eat most anything. He'll eat a piece of paper if you put a little sugar on it. They got a sweet tooth. They love sweet stuff."

That explains the Sugar Pops. Sugar Pops are basic. They go on the hook first to disguise it and make the carp pick it up. All baits are molded around Sugar Pops.

"We sell in the bait shop, I guess about five cases of Sugar Pops a week," Bob says.

Indeed, the bait shop, once the pawn shop, looks more like a grocery store, the shelves lined with exotic fare that fishermen mix together for their baits. They begin with a basic substance, usually Trout Chow, soybean meal, or millet, or a combination.

"The Trout Chow, some of 'em want it ground; some of 'em want half of it ground, half of it whole. We grind it for them," Bob says.

What they mix with the basic substance most keep to themselves.

Some use prunes, Bob says. "They use a tremendous amount of pineapple juice because it's sticky. It makes their bait stay together. I don't know how much pineapple juice we do sell. Sweet potatoes, cooked sweet potatoes. Apple sauce. Squash. Canned corn. They use all types of baby foods. I guess we sell 15 cases of baby food a week. Tomato ketchup, they use a lot of. And Kool-Aid. Jello. The cherry is the biggest seller, and strawberry.

"There's some flavorings, too, that we sell a tremendous amount of. They use vanilla flavoring, rum flavoring, butternut. It's crazy."

"I've seen people use some of the weirdest stuff you've ever seen," says Shell Teague, who helps run the lake. "French dressing. There are people who use likker in their bait. I've seen 'em pour beer in it. Sun Drop. I've seen likker work. Don't nobody tell the best bait they know. Different days, these carp will hit different things."

A bait that Shell has seen have a lot of success is Trout Chow, cherry Kool-Aid, pineapple juice and butternut flavoring with Minute Rice to make it break apart and puddle on the bottom so the carp will scoop it up without noticing the hook disguised with Sugar Pops. He's won some money on that combination himself.

"Oh yeah," Bob says. "Minute Rice. We sell an awful lot of that. They even use this Texas Pete hot sauce. We sell a lot of that.

"Some people say, like when the fish is pecking at the bait, they think if they put Texas Pete on it, the fish'll take off with it because it burns their mouth," Shell says. "I don't know if that's true or not."

"That's what they tell," Bob says. "I told you it's crazy."

The Waldenses

VALDESE   Even if you knew nothing about the history of Valdese, you'd know something was different about the town just from the street signs: Rodoret, Arnaud, Janavel, St. Germain, Martinat.

A French town in the hills of North Carolina?

Not exactly, although the services at Waldensian Presbyterian Church were conducted in French until 1922, and some of the older residents still speak French or a patois mixture of French and Italian.

Actually, the town's settlers came from Italy, from a series of remote valleys only 18 miles long and 14 miles wide in the Cottian Alps on the French border. Their ancestors were Protestant Christians who fled to those valleys to escape persecution by the Catholic church. They called themselves Waldenses, from the Vallis Dense, and they claimed to be members of the oldest evangelical Christian group on earth.

Waldenses trace their roots back more than a thousand years. They refused to accept the church in Rome and were declared heretics. When the pope decreed that only church officials could read and interpret the Bible and that all Bibles in the hands of others be destroyed, Waldenses set books of the Bible to memory and sent missionaries across the land disguised as traders.

In the Middle Ages the Waldensian valleys were repeatedly ravaged. Thousands of Waldenses were slaughtered for their beliefs and activities. Bubonic plague seriously depleted their numbers in 1630 and prompted the group to call upon Protestants in Geneva for leadership. The pastors who responded were French-speaking, thus introducing that language to the group, and in the valleys it remains the language in which worship services are conducted.

In 1686, Louis XIV, king of France, decided to crush the Waldenses once and for all. Troops were sent to the valleys. Their commander promised the Waldenses that if they surrendered their weapons as a symbol of loyalty, no harm would come to them. Once they had the weapons the troops began a massacre.

Little groups of Waldenses escaped, hid in the mountains, eventually came together and made their way into Switzerland. The massacre provoked outrage in England and other countries, and the king of England offered money and equipment to help the Waldenses regain their land. In 1689, a band of 800 Waldenses, using guerrilla tactics, defeated thousands of troops and retook their valleys, a feat proclaimed one of the greatest in military history by no less an

147

Waldensian Presbyterian Church maintains the old culture

authority than Napoleon. The Waldenses' victory is still celebrated as The Glorious Return.

For the next 160 years, the Waldenses suffered persecutions on a lesser scale, but those ended in 1848 when King Charles Albert granted full civil liberties.

Ironically, the coming of peace brought problems. Population boomed. The valleys couldn't support all the people. Hunger was common. Hopeless, some left for South America, others for New York and the American West.

Then a man who was president of a North Carolina land company with vast holdings in the mountains heard about their plight while traveling in Europe and concocted a scheme to help. His company, he told Waldensian leaders, would sell them on credit vast acreage for a new settlement in the mountains of North Carolina, and they could pay for it with money they made from the land.

Two farmers were sent to scout the land, but they found the first land shown them, in the rugged mountains of McDowell and Yancey counties, unacceptable. Another tract of 10,000 acres in lesser mountains east of Morganton was offered. One of the farmers found this rocky and mostly forested land acceptable; the other did not. But after they returned to the valley with their report, 13 families, with 29 members decided to accept the offer.

In May 1893, the group left by steamship for New York and arrived at its new wilderness home on May 29 by train on a dead-end section of track that the land company had persuaded the railroad to build from the nearby resort at Connelly Springs with the promise the Waldenses would be shipping out large amounts of lumber and bark for tanneries. The land company had built for the settlers several small wooden shacks and one large building, in which the whole group spent its first night.

Shortly after their arrival, the settlers formed a communal corporation and signed an agreement with the land company. For the 10,000 acres, a steam sawmill, cook stoves, wagons, a few cattle and a month's provisions for each family, the settlers agreed to pay $25,000 in 20 years at 5 percent interest. They had to get another loan for tools and mules.

Then they went about planting crops on the few rocky acres that had been cleared, clearing other land and trying to learn to operate the sawmill. Soon they were joined by other Waldensian settlers who had come earlier to other parts of the country, and 178 more arrived from the valleys in November.

Discontent quickly surfaced when the new settlers realized that the first group had taken the best farms near the railroad and their own lands were not as good. Some left for other areas. Some objected to the jobs they were assigned.

All faced hardship in the coming winter. Crops had been poor. The sawmill was barely able to produce enough lumber to build crude houses for the new arrivals. The settlers could see no way they could ever make enough from the land to repay the loan. They wouldn't even be able to pay the interest on it.

Some families with older children sent them off to nearby towns and cities to work as domestics. One girl worked in the home of a cotton mill superintendent, and leaders of the community talked him into opening a cotton mill in a barn they had built. The equipment he installed was antiquated. The settlers who worked there were able to make only a few cents a day. The mill did not last long.

By spring, the settlers realized something had to be done, and they sold half their land, the less desirable half, back to the land company, reducing their debt by $7,000.

Crops proved better that year, and the community even was able to sell a little lumber, but bickering and bitterness were tearing it apart, and by the end of that year, the Valdese Corporation decided to disband. It worked out a deal with the land company to absolve its debts and resell the land in tracts to individual settlers. Many families sent members away to other places to get jobs and send money home to pay for their land.

One who went away to work in hosiery mills, John Bobo Garrou, returned in a few years to use his experience and $345 he had accumulated to start his own mill. That mill, Alba-Waldensian, gave the town a viable economic basis and remains its largest employer.

Descendants of those early settlers have since melded into North Carolina life. Only one of the early settlers, Alex Guigou, who arrived as a small child, remains alive at 96. Few families of pure Waldensian ancestry remain in this town of 3,600. But the town's Waldensian heritage is far from forgotten.

The Waldenses joined with the Presbyterians soon after their arrival in Valdese, and the church they started building of native stone in 1896, Waldensian Presbyterian, has done much to preserve the heritage. The church started collecting artifacts of the early settlers in 1947, and in 1974, it erected a museum on Rodoret Street to house them.

The church also participates in the Waldensian Festival of the Glorious Return held by the town each August. This year's festival drew more than 12,000 people. For a month each summer, an outdoor drama that tells the story of the Waldenses, "From This Day Forward," is staged at the Old Colony Amphitheater on Church Street. The first house built by the settlers, the steam engine that ran their sawmill, and one of the colony's outdoor stone ovens have been preserved at the amphitheater.

The outdoor drama is staged Thursday through Sunday nights the last two weeks of July and the first two weeks of August. The festival is held the second Saturday in August. The Waldensian Museum is open Sundays 3–5 p.m., at other times by appointment. On days the drama is being performed, it is open 5–8:30 p.m.

Drive and Determination

VALDESE   He was not yet 23 when he left the valleys of his youth for good.

"He said he used to lie awake nights over in the old country thinking that something had to give," John Rostan Jr. says, remembering his father's stories.

The crowded agricultural valleys of the Waldenses in northern Italy offered no future for a young man, so in October 1903, John Rostan sailed for New York and got a job as a busboy in a restaurant. He didn't particularly like restaurant work but it gave him a foothold, and five years later he returned to the valleys and brought his sister back with him. With them came Irma Ghigo, 19, a family acquaintance who was coming to New York to live with her brother, Filippo.

Irma and Filippo's family operated a small bakery in the valleys and in 1910 Filippo started a bakery in New York. John, tired of the restaurant business, became his partner. Three months later, John married Irma. There was no honeymoon. He rushed to the ceremony from his bread deliveries and had to be up at 2 the next morning and on the street with his bread.

He detested the crowded streets, especially in winter when they were icy, and he hated the long flights of stairs he had to climb to make his deliveries. The bakery seemed to be getting nowhere. Competition was too strong. In the spring of 1915, John, then 34 and father of a 3-year-old son, Athos, realized once again that something had to give if he were ever going to make something of himself.

He talked with Filippo and they decided to sell the bakery and start anew in another place. They scouted areas near New York without finding an acceptable spot. Finally, they decided to move south to the mountains of North Carolina where a Waldensian settlement was becoming the town of Valdese. "At least we would be with our own people," John would say years later of the decision.

They arrived in May 1915, bought a lot on Main Street and began clearing it by hand. They hired a mason to erect a two-story building of stone and brick, 40 feet by 50, with a bakery on the first floor and living quarters for their two families upstairs. Their hearth-type oven, fed by coke, was built into one corner downstairs. By August, they had it in operation.

They baked the bread of the old country, long loaves, crusty on the outside, soft and coarse inside. But they had made one serious miscalculation. Most of the Waldensians were poor, couldn't afford

151

to buy bread and baked their own.

"There just was no market," says John Jr., who was born two and a half years after his family arrived in Valdese. "They had to change their type of baking and go to a pan-type bread that people called light bread. Dad started then to haul bread to Morganton. He would ship it by rail, and he would hobo over there to sell it."

The hoboing ended when John caught his pants leg while jumping from the train and would have been dragged to his death if the fabric hadn't torn. After that, he walked the eight miles to Morganton, picked up his bread at the station, delivered it in baskets and walked back.

With early profits, he bought a horse and wagon, but that proved impractical and he reluctantly ordered a hard-tired International truck with a hand crank on one side. He used to love to recall the adventures he had with that truck before he mastered it.

That truck almost caused him to give up the bakery business. It was balky about cranking and one bitterly cold morning, after he'd tried dozens of times to crank it without success, John swore that if it didn't crank on the next turn, he was quitting forever and going back to New York to wait tables for the rest of his life. As if destiny itself had a hand on the crank, the engine coughed and caught on the next turn.

In 1918, John did go back to waiting tables. Supply shortages brought by World War I forced the bakery to close. Filippo took a job in a cotton mill. John went back to New York. There he got caught in the great flu epidemic. Irma left her two sons behind with relatives and went to New York to nurse him back to health. In the spring of 1919, they returned and reopened the bakery, followed by a new dough mixing machine that John had bought in New York.

In the early '20s, roads started opening up in western North Carolina and John saw potential in them. Almost every little town had a bakery then and John knew he would have to overcome that competition if his bakery were to grow. He started by buying out the bakery in Hickory, then moved on to Granite Falls, Marion, Lenoir and Shelby.

By 1929, the bakery in Valdese had outgrown its first building and a new plant was built on the east end of Main Street, which three years later would become U.S. 64. Filippo had sold his interest in the bakery to an employee, Earl Searcy, in 1925 and retired to raise grapes and chickens at his house on Main Street.

John ran the bakery and kept pushing to expand it. In 1930, he joined the Quality Bakers of America Co-operative, which developed the Sunbeam brand in the '40s. By 1957, he had built the first plant in the world designed to produce batter-whipped Sunbeam bread, and his territory for selling it covered all of western North Carolina.

John remained president of the bakery until his death in 1972, a month short of his 92nd birthday. Until shortly before his death, he walked to work every morning from the modest brick house he built across the street from the plant he built in 1929. His widow, now 95, still lives there.

John Jr. became president of the bakery after his father's death. He and his older brother, Athos, now retired, grew up in the bakery. As children, they spoke French and it was from the bakery workers that they learned English, including, John Jr. says with a smile, more than a few cuss words.

"We were brought up to work," he says. "Whatever we were able to do we did back from the time we were just kids."

John, who graduated from Davidson College as a chemistry major, always knew he'd be going back to the bakery.

"I didn't have any other thoughts," he says, then laughs. "I didn't know what I was getting into either. I pulled every job there is to be done, one job to the next as soon as I was able to do it. Yeah, I worked a bread route, too."

After the death of Earl Searcy in 1970, the Rostan family bought his interest and now owns all but a few shares of the bakery. It will remain a family business, John Jr. says. Athos' son, Athos Jr., is vice president and director of sales. John Jr.'s son, Jim, is executive vice president. His son, John III, is vice president of administration.

As a family business Waldensian Bakeries releases no figures on sales, production and profits, but it employs more than 550 people with an annual payroll of more than $10 million and keeps a fleet of 275 vehicles on the road. It makes Sunbeam, Roman Meal and Waldensian Heritage bread and rolls and sells them in 50 counties of western North Carolina, Virginia, Georgia, Tennessee and South Carolina. Its cakes are sold across the eastern United States. Its plant, expanded several times, now covers an area the size of four football fields, has a capacity of producing more than a million pounds of bread a day and perfumes the air of Valdese around the clock.

John Jr. sits in the office building of that plant and contemplates what led his father to build such a business.

"He just had drive and determination. I think the poverty that these people in Valdese went through gave them real determination. It was succeed or else. It was just determination and hard work that led him to do it. That's it. Hard work and determination."

Bocce

VALDESE   "It can be spelled b-o-c-c-i-e or b-o-c-c-e," Ernest Jahier says with a mischievous grin. "Not b-o-t-c-h-y."

Just pronounce it botchy.

A game, bocce is. A very popular game among Italians. Especially Italian men. In Italian, boccia means ball. Bocce involves nine balls, hard ones: eight of them 4½ inches in diameter, four red, four black, one 2½ inches in diameter, a neutral color.

The game is very simple on the surface. The little ball, called the pallino, is rolled onto a court. Then two teams vie to roll or toss the bigger balls as close to the pallino as possible. One point is scored for each large ball closer to the target ball than the other team's closest ball.

Under the surface, experienced players will tell you, the game is quite complex.

"After the first ball is rolled," says Ernest, "most anything goes. You can knock your opponent's ball away. You can push your ball closer. You can move the target ball."

Some are finesse players, who specialize in kissing the pallino with their balls. Others are spockers, who toss fearsome balls designed to send their opponents' good shots on long trips.

Bocce has been played in Valdese since the first settlers arrived from the Waldensian valleys of northern Italy in 1893.

"Bocce was their only means of recreation," Ernest says. "They wasted no time in building a court."

A court can be a variety of sizes. Usually they are from 65 to 80 feet long, 10 to 14 feet wide, a hard surface, usually clay, enclosed with wooden walls at least 10 inches high. The court on Valdese's Main Street, between the Waldensian Presbyterian Church and the Citgo station, is only 62 feet long because a utility pole was in the way.

"In Valdese, we had seven courts at one time," says Ernest. "Now we have only three. Rarely used. I hate to say it."

Ernest learned to play bocce as a youngster because his parents had a court in their back yard in New York. In those days tradition restricted the game to men.

Ernest's parents had brought him to New York from the Waldensian valleys in 1914, when he was six. His grandmother had immigrated to Valdese in 1896. Ernest used to spend summers with her and watch the local bocce players at their sport.

"I wasn't allowed to play," he says. "I vowed someday I would come back and play."

Little did he know that by the time he retired and moved to Valdese in 1970, few people would be playing the game.

Ernest was accustomed to New York, where bocce courts abound, even inside some restaurants, and spirited tournaments are regularly held. In Valdese, he found only one tournament, held by Les Phare Des Alps, a men's club, on the Fourth of July, an event from which women were forbidden until five years ago.

"That's when they let us come to the sanctum sanctorum," says Ernest's wife, Frances, who is of Yugoslavian ancestry. "Had to take your shoes off and bow three times. We started to rebel. We said, 'What goes on in there? Do they have dancing girls or what?'"

Women rarely play in that tournament, but some do play in the tournament held each August during the town's Waldensian Festival of the Glorious Return, and this year's winning team included a young woman, April Phillips. One player came all the way from Manteo to participate.

Ironically, Ernest believes that his attempts to revive bocce in Valdese have had greater effect outside the town.

For four weeks each summer, Ernest, who's an enthusiastic 77, teaches the game to visitors on the court at Old Colony Amphitheater before the outdoor drama that tells the story of the Waldenses, "From This Day Forward," begins each night.

"It's beginning to take root in different parts of North Carolina because people who come to see the drama, if they're interested in bocce, I give them a paper in which they're told how to build a court and how to play."

A court can be built fairly easily and inexpensively, he points out.

"After that, there's no cost whatsoever. No green fees, no caddies, no clubs of any kind."

Already, he knows of courts that have been built in Durham, Hickory and Spindale.

"Bocce is not a Johnny-come-lately game," he says. "Bocce was played 5,000 years ago by the early Egyptians. They passed it on to the Greeks, who passed it to the Romans, and the Romans gave it to the Waldenses. Bocce is played throughout the world. The game is very popular among the Waldenses in Italy."

But not so popular among the younger people of Waldensian ancestry in Valdese.

"The young people nowadays have different interests. They have other means of recreation. It's a shame because bocce is as much a part of the Waldensian heritage as the patois, but then that's not being spoken by many young people anymore either."

The Sausage Makers

VALDESE   You'd think that a town settled by Waldensians of northern Italy, as Valdese was, a town as proud of its heritage as Valdese is, would have lots of Waldensian food available. But try to find a restaurant in town that serves any and you're out of luck.

The only time you can get a traditional Waldensian meal of soutisso, cabbage, potatoes and crusty bread is on festival day in August at Waldensian Presbyterian Church.

But if you want to cook soutisso yourself, you need only search out Walsh Market. A big sign by U.S. 64 on the west side of town directs the way a short distance down Hoyle Street. Walsh Market is a neighborhood grocery with an old-time meat market where David Walsh, third generation soutisso maker, is found trimming hams to make the lone Waldensian food specialty to be found in town.

"It's got salt and pepper and garlic," says David, "and we can't tell you the rest. It's real spicy. It's not hot but it's got a unique flavor."

Ham is the only meat in it, trimmed of almost all fat, coarsely ground, mixed with seasonings and stuffed into natural casings to make fat sausages.

"It's a dinner sausage," says David's father, Ralph, who once made the sausage himself. "You boil it. Most people just boil it with potatoes and carrots and make a whole meal in one pot. Some people use cabbage.

"Regular Italian sausage has a lot of fat in it. You can fry it. This is not made to fry. It's made to boil. The old Waldenses used to put saltpeter and about three times the salt that we do and they would cure it to keep it over the winter, put it in the attic. But there's no preservatives in this."

The Walshes have been making Waldensian sausage longer than anybody in Valdese, but they are not Waldensian. Ralph's father, Robert, called Rob, was born in Wilkes County and went to Rhodhiss in Caldwell County as a young man to get a job in a mill. There he married, and after losing job and home in the great flood of 1916, he moved to Valdese and got a job in the cotton mill store.

"He would go around over town and take orders and go back in the afternoon with a wheelbarrow and deliver 'em," says Ralph. "Then they migrated to a horse and wagon, then to a Model T."

When Rob saved a little money, he bought out the meat market at the Carolina Store for $80 and began operating it. That's where he began making soutisso sometime in the '20s.

156

Ralph Walsh, right, and son David

"Oscar Pascal's mother—he's the chief of police of Valdese—gave Dad this recipe," says Ralph.

Local visitors to the old country have since checked the recipe and found it to be authentic, he says.

Ralph's daddy, who later owned and operated several markets in Valdese, made several other specialties as well as Waldensian sausage.

"Gosh," says Ralph, "he used to make beef tongue loaf, chicken loaf, homemade sousemeat. Lord, I don't know what all he did make. But, of course, livermush got to be the big thing. He started making livermush, must've been in the late '30s.

"The first potful was made at home in a black bean pot that set over the eye of the cook stove. Mama made the first run and I'm pretty sure my grandmother's recipe was the one used. A couple of weeks of that and they couldn't keep it made, so they got a pot that covered two eyes of the cook stove. That got too little after a couple of years."

Ralph, who's 59, grew up working in his daddy's store, but when he was 34 he went to Hickory and opened a store of his own. In 1965, he returned to Valdese and opened this market in what had been a service station and tire recapping shop. His dad had sold his store a couple of years earlier with the idea of retiring but soon returned to work for the man to whom he'd sold the store.

"He couldn't stand retirement," says Ralph.

So when Ralph opened his store, his daddy came to work for him, and Ralph built a big, gas-fired black pot into the corner of his meat market so he could continue to make his livermush.

"When Dad got so old he couldn't stir the livermush pot, he taught David," says Ralph.

"We make about 425 pounds at a time," David says. "We usually make it twice a week in the wintertime and once a week in the summer. You sell a lot more in the winter."

"This livermush is known all over the United States," says Ralph. "In fact we call it world famous. If it's been everywhere they say it has, it's been to Iran, Hawaii, Alaska, I don't know where all.

"Where does your daughter take it back to?" he asks a customer who has come from Morganton to get some.

"Richmond," she says.

David makes all the livermush and soutisso now, using the recipes his grandfather gave him, still doing it exactly as his grandfather did. His grandfather died in 1979 at age 85.

"He was working here the day he had his heart failure," says Ralph, who has himself had two heart attacks and isn't able to work much anymore.

David is 33. He went to Lenoir Rhyne College, got a degree in business administration, then decided to return to work with his father.

"He was born in the store and I was born in the store," says Ralph. "His kids, we raised 'em in a pasteboard box up front when they were little. We're all born and raised in a store."

David and his wife, Phyllis, who also works at the store as cashier, have a son, Chris, and a daughter, Cindy.

It's too early yet to tell whether Chris might continue his family's tradition of making Waldensian sausage and livermush. He's only 10.

"I kinda hoped David would pass it down to the fourth generation," says Ralph, "but Chris, whether he'd be interested in it, I don't know."

Passage

Cluttered is the way to describe the highway on its eight-mile run from Valdese to Morganton. A conglomeration of homes and businesses, junkyards and construction lots lines the patched and bumpy roadway.

Hardly a scenic sight.

But off to the left, the South Mountains loom, serene in late-summer haze.

Morganton is famous as the site of the 1833 hanging of Frankie Silver, a jealous woman who killed her husband and buried his heart under the front doorstep. She was the first woman executed in North Carolina, and a song about her evil deed, "Frankie and Johnny," became a long-lasting hit.

The town claims two famous residents—former Sen. Sam Ervin, who gained wide attention for conducting the Watergate hearings, and Joann Denton, a self-proclaimed witch who won international fame after being arrested for correctly predicting the date of a woman's death.

The highway divides on Morganton's east side. The new road, the bypass, swings south past glitzy shopping centers and the huge plants, Nos. 3 and 5, of Drexel Heritage Furniture Co. Plant 5 has enjoyed 2 million hours without a lost-time accident.

The old road continues through downtown—split onto one-way streets, Union westbound, Meeting eastbound—squeezing the stuccoed Burke County Courthouse with its ornate cupola between the two. Built of locally cut stone in 1835, the courthouse withstood a raid by Yankee troops 30 years later, was remodeled in 1901 and is now undergoing renovation once again.

The old road rejoins the new beside the shaded, spacious lawns of the hilltop campus of the North Carolina School for the Deaf in the southwestern part of town, then passes the even more spacious, but austere, campus of Western Piedmont Community College before having its fifth and final encounter with Interstate 40.

Now the highway heads south into the mountains toward Rutherfordton, 30 miles away.

The community of Brindletown, once a gold-mining center, is apparently divided over the spelling of its name. The community center spells it Brindletown, the volunteer fire department Brendletown. The North Carolina Gazetteer goes with the community center.

This section of the highway is lightly traveled with none of the touristy trappings so common to other major mountain roads. The South Mountains have been largely undiscovered by outsiders, and those who have found them failed to get much of a foothold. A cluster of buildings meant to be the center of a mountain homesite development stands forlorn and overgrown with weeds by the side of the road.

Mostly, the highway clings to the valleys, following creeks through bottomlands lush with corn and pasture, past neat, tin-roofed, frame houses with front porches set off by flowers where people take their leisure on summer Sunday afternoons. But 13 miles south of Morganton it enters McDowell County for a four-mile stretch and becomes steep and curvy as it passes through a gap in the mountains, both sides of the highway lined with deep woods. Small signs point the way to summer camps.

Entering Rutherford County, the highway takes to bottomland again, passing large patches of sorghum cane growing amid the corn and pastures. Molasses makers abide here. In the distance, whole mountains struggle to recover after being denuded by timber cutters, their sides marked by the red slashes of crude and eroding roads.

On through the community of Cane Creek, past a road that leads to Sunshine, the home of a man who repairs clocks ("Pendulum type only") and Brittain Presbyterian Church, organized eight years before this country declared its independence, the highway goes, leaving the mountains behind temporarily. It crosses the Second Broad River and passes a big sign that says "Jesus Saves" before it joins U.S. Highway 74 at Ruth, a town that stole the first part of the name of the county in which it is located.

Joined with 74, the highway heads west again, into the land of kudzu. It would be easy to get the impression that kudzu was taking over this part of the world. It covers the roadsides, climbs over trees, signs, power lines and anything else in its way, even tries to creep over the highway itself. A selective, chemical frost brought by massive spraying, has left it brown in great patches, incongruous amid the lushness all around.

Greater mountains lie ahead. Now the traffic is heavy and slow with gawkers, particularly on weekends in summer and fall. The roadside bristles with antique shops, stands selling sourwood honey, fresh apple cider and mountain chow-chow. Signs tout the glories of campgrounds, gift shops, restaurants, lodges, motels, mountain attractions and time-share resorts.

Beyond an unnamed spot that declares itself "Pumpkin Center of the South" (only a single field of pumpkins can be seen nearby), the highway begins to climb again and soon meets the Rocky Broad River, which is very rocky but not so broad, clear and swift and alive with tubers on a hot Sunday afternoon.

Around a sharp curve, a sign welcomes visitors to Hickory Nut Gorge, "Deep Gateway Through the Blue Ridge." The resort towns of Lake Lure and Chimney Rock lie just ahead. The highway, which began in tourist land some 440 miles back, has returned to it.

Tent Meeting

MORGANTON   It was not the kind of crowd to warm an evangelist's heart. Fewer than three dozen people, many of them children, were scattered among the 200 folding chairs under fluorescent street lights inside the big blue and white vinyl tent.

But Brother Gary hadn't let that influence his preaching. Whether he was preaching to a single person or a multitude, he gave his all. When he got wound up, really going good, his forehead beading with sweat under his glistening, swept-back Elvis-of-the-'50s hairdo, he took off his coat and hopped off the red-carpeted stage so he could pace in the woodshavings, get close to his congregation and tell them what they came to hear.

"You can't fool with God. You need to get down to business with the Lord. Say, 'Lord, it don't matter. I want to get straight with you.'"

Anybody who'd been to a tent meeting before knew that the climax was imminent, that Brother Gary was getting down to the altar call. His voice softened. "Now everybody that would like to come and kneel down and pray, come and kneel down and get saved, I want you to come on now. How many would like to see somebody's soul saved here tonight?"

Every hand went up, and Brother Gary began telling how he'd been saved at a tent meeting himself when he was a boy of nine.

"It would be worth this whole revival meeting if just one soul would get saved here tonight," he said, concluding his story.

Already, his wife, Gayle, was playing softly on the organ. His daughters, Laura, eight, and Jennifer, five, both in frilly white dresses, had risen from their seats on the stage. Softly, they began singing with their mother.

"Take your burden to the Lord and leave it there . . ."

Brother Gary sang, too, his Elvis-like voice trembling, pausing now and then to say, "Would you come? Would you pray with me?"

Nobody came and Brother Gary began to pray alone, beseeching: "Lord, if there's anybody here that needs you, Father, in Jesus name, give them deliverance tonight. May they turn from the old and turn to the new."

After repeated pleas, it became obvious that this would not be a night for turning, for soul saving, but Brother Gary couldn't let go, couldn't let himself bring the service to a close for some reason.

"I believe somebody prayed with me tonight," he said. "I really do. Does anybody have a need?"

When nobody responded this time, he singled out a frail old woman.

"Sister, come up here," he said. "I want to pray for that eye."

162

Evangelist Gary Posey

Gary Posey, who is 34, grew up in a mill section in Greenville, S.C. When Gary was a teenager, his daddy, Bill, a maintenance man at a carpet company, had a prayer meeting at his home and got saved with such fervor that he soon took up radio preaching.

The whole family began attending a small Pentecostal Holiness church, where, at 17, Gary became Sunday School superintendent and set new records for attendance. After high school, Gary joined the Air Force and was sent to the Philippines where he began working with evangelical missionaries in his off-duty hours. By the time he was reassigned to Mississippi, he'd decided preaching would be his life's work.

Shortly after his return, he married his high school sweetheart, who'd played organ at the Pentecostal church, and in Mississippi he started holding revivals at small churches, but he knew that he was not being led to pastor a church, not then.

"The Lord began to speak to me about the tent ministry, began to lay that upon my heart," he says. "I just felt that's what He wanted me to do."

By saving all the money he could, taking special offerings at the churches where he preached, and with help from his daddy and brothers, he was able to get an old tent and a '56 Ford truck to haul it in before he got out of the Air Force. "It was a wonderful blessing how the Lord brought things together for us," he says.

He held his first meeting in his hometown after his discharge.

"We had over 250 the first night," he says. "We had quite a number that came that were saved, some we prayed for. It was a blessing."

He took his tent meetings all over the South before the Lord directed him to start Victory Temple in an old school in Concord. He stayed off the road three years establishing the temple and a daily radio ministry over WLXN in Lexington. But the tent ministry kept calling him and six years ago he took it up again, this time venturing no more than a couple of hundred miles from home so he can keep up his temple and radio work.

This was his first time in Morganton. He'd come 17 days earlier, bringing his 100-by-50-foot tent in a tilt cab truck, pulling the travel trailer his family would live in for the next three weeks behind his worn Lincoln Continental. It took two days to set up the tent at the Burke County Farmers Market on U.S. 64, where traveling tent evangelists pay no rent. Two more days were required to get the power turned on, rent the Porta-Johns, haul in a load of wood shavings to keep down dirt and mud, put together the stage, set up the big speakers to amplify his voice, the organ for his wife to play, the drums for his brother, Ricky (who can sing just like Elvis), the white pulpit with the red cross on front that his daddy built for him, and the signs out by the highway that say "Victory Revival Crusade With Evangelist Gary Posey, Now in Progress, 7:45 nightly."

This was the 14th night since the revival opened, the 12th night of services (no services are held on Sunday when Brother Gary is back at the temple). Only two more nights to go, and Brother Gary was sure that attendance, which had been averaging about 50 a night, he said, would pick up dramatically.

After all, he was convinced that God had a special feeling for tent meetings. "It always seemed like the Lord would really bless a tent meeting," he would say later. "I feel like the Spirit of the Lord really moves under a tent more than any other place."

But this night the Spirit was frustratingly slow in moving. The woman that Brother Gary called forward was wrinkled and bent. She wore a long green skirt printed with tiny yellow flowers, a white blouse, red shoes and white socks. Three heavy-set women escorted her to the front.

The woman had come to an earlier service and asked Brother Gary to pray for the cataracts on her eye. She'd pronounced the eye healed that night, but before this service she'd mentioned to Brother Gary that she was having a little blurred vision. He wanted to give the eye a second shot of prayer.

"Pray with us for this grandma tonight," he asked his congregation, then placed his hands on the woman's forehead. "Lord, we ask you to touch this eye, just give her perfect sight in it, Lord. I believe you're going to touch it. We pray victory in Christ's name, right NOW! Oh, thank you, Jesus. Thank you, Jesus."

While he prayed, his wife played the organ and she and her daughters sang, "Somebody touched me," the elder daughter, Laura, keeping time on a tambourine.

"Now look real good," Brother Gary told the woman. "Is it clearing?"

She spoke excitedly, words the congregation couldn't hear.

"Bless your heart," Brother Gary said, laughing joyously. "Well, the Lord's touched it. I believe that's why. You can just praise God tonight."

Before the woman returned to her seat, Brother Gary also prayed for one of the heavy women who'd hobbled to the front with her.

"Somebody help me pray for these legs tonight," he said. "Poor ol' thing has to walk around on that cane.

"Sister," he said when he finished praying, "just go ahead and see if you can pick 'em up. Just work 'em a little.

"Praise God!," he cried as she hopped on one foot. "I believe you're going to find the Lord's loosened 'em up for you."

Next, he prayed for a woman who wanted to quit smoking, then for a timid little girl who was reluctantly pushed forward by her mother to have Brother Gary pray over a tiny sore on the girl's arm.

"We're running a little later tonight than we ordinarily do," Brother Gary said as his wife and daughters still played and sang in the background, "but I believe the Lord's still working."

Behind him, his younger daughter, Jennifer, came forward on the stage carrying a small white plastic wastebasket. Brother Gary turned to her and grinned.

"What you doin', sweetheart? Oh, you feel the spirit moving you, don't you," he said, taking the basket. "I think the offering last night was $18. I had to fill up my car last night and it took $13. I'm not complaining but I do need God to help us. I'm not going to let the financial burden hinder me. I know the Lord will make a way for me. We do thank you and appreciate your support, even if it's a nickel or a dime. I'll give you a receipt for it if you need it."

His wife brought up the organ music. The whole family starting singing, and most in the congregation came forward to drop something into the basket.

"Thank you, Jesus!" cried Brother Gary. "Somebody say, 'Praise the Lord!' Hallelujah!"

The Man on the Gate

LAKE LURE   This is one of his afternoons on the gate. Saturdays and Sundays, the busy days, are always his afternoons.

The cars keep coming, sometimes lining up three or four at a time. They have been drawn by the signs advertising the famous Bottomless Pools, an unusual series of deep holes, one of them 59 feet, dug along a fault line in solid granite by whirlpools along Pool Creek.

"Want to see the pools?" he keeps asking the people inside the cars. "It's 50 cents each."

It's unlikely that any of the tourists realizes that the dapper little man wearing a red bow tie and taking their half dollars is a millionaire whom presidents and governors have called by his first name, or that he more than anybody else is responsible for making the resort town of Lake Lure what it is today.

"I just do this for the exercise," Lee Powers says, pocketing the bills from a carload of visitors. "As long as you've got all the money you need, you can do what you want. There's no need to worry."

Lee Powers owns the Bottomless Pools and 350 mountain acres surrounding them. At one time he owned nearly six miles of waterfront on Lake Lure, where 100-foot lots now sell for as much as $20,000, and although he's sold some of that, he still owns a considerable amount. He has Treasury Bonds that pay more than 16 percent. But when he came to Lake Lure in 1931, Lee was broke and so was Lake Lure.

Lake Lure was a dream that almost came true. It was conceived by a doctor from Kansas City named Lucius Morse. Shortly after the turn of the century, Dr. Morse came to the mountains in hopes of curing his tuberculosis. He settled for a while in Hendersonville, and in exploring the nearby countryside, he came upon Chimney Rock, an unusual formation that has attracted people for hundreds of years.

When Dr. Morse first saw it, people were climbing a steep trail to stand atop it, holding onto a rope attached to a sure-footed mule. Dr. Morse and his wealthy brothers bought the rock, built a road to it and opened it as a tourist attraction in 1916. That was just a beginning for Dr. Morse. He saw Chimney Rock as part of a bigger thing.

He wanted to build a huge resort for the rich, a resort built around a big lake with several golf courses, stables, riding trails, a plush hotel with a big beach, expensive waterfront homes. In the early '20s he formed a group of investors and began acquiring land. He

166

Lee Powers

bought 210 different tracts, a total of nearly 9,000 acres. He hired engineers to build a dam and hydroelectric plant on the Rocky Broad River. The dam was finished in 1926, and the deep, clear lake that backed up behind it, the lake Dr. Morse hoped would lure the rich, covered 1,500 acres.

On an upper cove of the lake a huge beach was built, along with a Mediterranean-style hotel, a marina and a complex for offices and shops. But before the resort could really begin operating, before the golf courses were built or any of the rich had bought waterfront lots, the Great Depression set in, and Dr. Morse and his group went bankrupt.

"I look at Dr. Morse the way I would Columbus," says Lee. "Columbus had to have a lot of guts to make that trip. It wasn't an intelligent thing to do."

When Lee arrived in Lake Lure, Dr. Morse was out of the picture, retreated to his original dream, Chimney Rock. The big lake resort— all but the hotel, which had been developed separately—had fallen to creditors. One had foreclosed on the dam and lake, another on the land surrounding it. Lee was sent as an agent of the company that had foreclosed on the land. His primary job was to liquidate it.

Lee was born in Tennessee, grew up mostly in Mobile and Birmingham. His father was a contractor who later moved to Charleston and Asheville and passed his trade on to his son.

"When I was 15 my father took me to one of his foremen and said, "I want you to teach this boy the carpentry trade,'" Lee recalls.

As a young man, he went out on his own in real estate and building, had some successes but also went broke a couple of times before he was hired to liquidate Lake Lure.

In this new job, he faced a mess. Trying to save the resort, the developers had incorporated part of it in 1929, and issued $250,000 in municipal bonds, the receipts from which were promptly lost. All sorts of problems had to be resolved.

Lee's big job was to sell land when few people could afford to buy it, but beyond that he had several other jobs—operating the beach, the boat landing, the Bottomless Pools, renting out space in the office and shop building and running the hotel and dining room on the second floor.

He went about solving the problems methodically and gradually he worked them out. He even began selling land. Slowly. A waterfront lot here, another there, never getting more than $500 for them. Before the 10 years he had to liquidate the property was up, he was selling land for $10 an acre. His commissions all went to buy land of his own.

By the time his job as liquidator was over, he had bought the Bottomless Pools and built himself a house by the creek below the falls that created the pools.

"When I came, I didn't intend to stay," he says.

But stay he did, starting a construction company that built many of the houses around the lake as more prosperous times came, dealing in real estate—and guiding the town. He helped the town out of its indebtedness and later he worked out arrangements for the town to buy the lake, the dam and the power plant for $390,000. The town now sells the power it generates for $600,000 a year. But despite all he did, Lee never was a town official.

"I learned many years ago to stay in the background. Don't get out in front 'cause you'll get in trouble. It's better not to run the town."

His interest in politics was strong, though, and he became a force in the state Democratic party, serving on commissions under several governors. He's been to six national Democratic conventions, four as a delegate, and he's known Presidents Roosevelt, Kennedy and Johnson and every governor for the past half century.

Lake Lure is now a popular and prosperous resort. The lake is alive with boaters, fishermen and water skiers, the shore lined with cottages and homes. The town-operated beach attracts a lot of tourists. A developer has bought the old hotel and is elegantly refurbishing it for year-around operation. Another company has achieved much of Dr. Morse's dream with golf courses and expensive condominiums on one section of the lake. And over it all, Lee Powers reigns as patriarch.

"They'll tell you I've done more for Lake Lure than anybody," he says during a lull at the gate to the Bottomless Pools. "It's not what I did for Lake Lure, it's what Lake Lure did for me, because everything I did, I came out on it. The day I came over here, I made money from then on. I've never borrowed a dollar since I've been in Lake Lure.

"My idea of a successful person is one who makes the right decision 51% of the time. I made the right decision about 80% of the time. Let me tell you something, though. I worked. I didn't fool around. You've got to work to accumulate something."

He is 85 now, and he has overcome some health problems, including a bout with cancer some years back.

"I don't fool with alcohol," he says. "I quit smoking 40 years ago. I walk two miles every day. I've always kept busy and had something to be interested in, and that's what makes your life worthwhile. I still do have things I'm interested in and want to do. I think that's what keeps me going."

Another car pulls up. Lee jumps quickly off his chair.

"Want to see the pools?" he says.

Tenders of the Wonders

CHIMNEY ROCK   Just above Lake Lure, two of North Carolina's great natural wonders overlook U.S. 64.

One, Chimney Rock, is easily accessible to anybody willing to part with $5. The other, Bat Cave, is hardly accessible at all but can be seen with patience and luck.

Chimney Rock, a huge pillar of stone rising out of the mountainside at the base of sheer cliffs, probably received its name because early settlers thought it looked like a smokestack, especially with early morning mist rising from it, but some say it was because Indians used it as a platform for sending smoke signals. It has been operated as a tourist attraction for a century, but it has been an intriguing, even enchanted place for much longer.

Cherokee Indians believed a ghost tribe they called The Little People lived on the dramatic granite cliffs of Chimney Rock Mountain. Indians weren't the only ones to see ghosts there. Early settlers reported seeing swarms of ghostly figures playing about the mountain, and in 1811 newspapers reported a heavenly cavalry battle, complete with sound, above Chimney Rock, witnessed by several people.

In 1880, Jerome Freeman bought the mountain from a land company, built a trail to the rock and constructed wooden steps to the top. He opened it to the public in 1885. Seventeen years later, he sold the mountain to Lucius Morse, a St. Louis doctor who came to the mountains hoping to cure his tuberculosis. Dr. Morse built a road to the rock and hired a local contractor, Guilford Nanney, to build new stairways and trails, not only to the top of the rock, but across the mountain to Hickory Nut Falls, a spectacular waterfall spilling 404 feet off the mountains top before cascading to the river. He also built a trail back along the cliff face, a 45-minute hike each way. Dr. Morse reopened the mountain with its new features on July 4, 1916.

Three years later, Guilford Nanney completed the Cliff Dwellers Inn on a perch beside the rock, and it became a big honeymooning spot before it had to be torn down in 1949 when more changes were made. This time workers tunneled 198 feet inside the mountain and used eight tons of dynamite to blast a shaft 258 feet up so that an elevator could be installed.

In place of the Cliff Dwellers Inn, the Sky Lounge, a gift shop, snack bar and viewing area, was built. The original Sky Lounge burned on Labor Day, 1981, and when a new one was built, the huge timbers that frame it were set in place by helicopter.

Lucius Morse died in 1946, and Chimney Rock is now owned by his grandson, Lucius III, a St. Louis businessman. From Chimney Rock, the church graveyard where Dr. Morse is buried can be seen on a hillside overlooking Lake Lure, which Dr. Morse also built.

Most visitors to the park take the elevator to the Sky Lounge, climb steps onto the rock, where to the east they can see 75 miles beyond Lake Lure into the Piedmont and to the west the entire length of Hickory Nut Gorge. Then they walk down through a system of trails, decks and stairways, so that they may see such spots as Pulpit Rock, the Grotto, the Subway, the Needle's Eye—150 steep steps straight through a narrow fault in the rock—and Moonshiner's Cave, a fissure cave where moonshiners once actually concocted their illicit brew.

From the wide windows of the Sky Lounge, Hazel Nelon, the gift shop clerk (her picture was in National Geographic in 1941 when she was 14, handhooking rugs with her mother in Bear Wallow) can almost look down at her life.

"My husband, Sid, he was born and raised about six miles this way, and I was born and raised about six miles that way," she says.

From the window, she can see the mountainsides her husband timbered, the flat spots he pushed off with bulldozers, the hardware store the two of them ran for 17 years, the place where they raised their three children, all now grown, the hollows where she and her husband hunted and the coves on Lake Lure where they caught whopper bass.

"I don't think there's any place any better anywhere than here," she says. "We went to Minnesota one time. We were going to be farmers, but, my Lord, I cried days and nights I got so homesick. I had to be back in the mountains. I been around a lot, but I'll take this place any ol' day."

A couple of miles up the Rocky Broad River from the entrance to Chimney Rock is a rusty steel bridge built in Greensboro in 1926. One side is blocked by a wooden fence, the other by a high steel-wire fence. Signs warn against trespassing.

Near the bridge, at one of her rental picnic tables, Sarah Lawter is hand chopping cabbage in a metal dishpan.

"No, not making kraut," she says. "Chow-chow. I'm a hillbilly. I like cabbage in my chow-chow. I'm going to make some kraut, though. Have to wait till the moon's right for that. It has a tendency to get soft if you don't make it under the right moon. New moon. That's when you make kraut. Don't make it on the full moon. It's still in. That's why I'm not making no kraut."

The bridge leads to a trail that goes up Blue Rock Mountain to Bat Cave, believed to be the largest fissure cave on earth. Most caves are caused by water seeping through limestone, but fissure caves are faults in the stone innards of the earth. Bat Cave is massive and has yet to be fully mapped. Its main room is 85 feet high and more than 300 feet long.

The cave, which is privately owned, has been abused by visitors who have littered and defiled it and driven away most of the bats that once inhabited it. Since 1980, the North Carolina Nature Conservancy has held jurisdiction over the cave and is trying to preserve its delicate plant and animal life. The conservancy allows only a few limited groups to visit the cave each year (for information write Box 815, Chapel Hill 27514).

Sarah, who lives across the road from the blockaded bridge to Bat Cave, runs a fruit stand and rents picnic tables beside it. Her husband, Arthur, is caretaker for the New York woman who owns Bat Cave plus a private school and summer home nearby. While he works, Sarah watches to see that nobody slips up to the cave.

"Oh, you have a lot of trouble," she says. "In fact, they prosecuted five last year. Lot of 'em wants to go in there and steal wild plants and ginseng and things like that—outside people. We don't have no trouble out of local people."

Her husband, a mountain man, often drives the highway looking for cars parked by the river, indicating that people may be on the mountain at the caves. He can be fearsome with trespassers.

"You should hear him say, 'Can you not read?'" Sarah says with a laugh. "It's young ones gives most of the trouble. That's why children nowadays are in prison, because they don't listen to their parents or pay attention to what's right and wrong. You can't tell some of 'em nothin'."

She stops chopping to wave at the annoying insects swarming about her dishpanful of cabbage.

"They should've called this Gnat Cave instead of Bat Cave," she says.

Apples and Education

HENDERSONVILLE   Orchards appear as U.S. 64 begins the climb up the mountains from Bat Cave to Hendersonville. By the time the highway reaches the continental divide, 2,260 feet, at Edneyville, it is lined with apple trees, roadside stands and packing houses, and in late summer and early fall the air is apple perfumed. Big trucks, lumbering under mountainous loads of apples, often clog traffic on this stretch of highway.

Edneyville is the center of North Carolina's apple country. Henderson County grows 80 percent of the state's apples, some eight million bushels a year, making it the seventh largest apple producing county in the nation. If the orchards by the highway, bowing under the burden of fruit, are any indication, this will be another bountiful year. But looks can be deceiving.

"This is a sad year for us," says Odell Barnwell. "This will be the sorriest crop we've had since '56, and we didn't have nothin' that year."

"We had hail," says his wife, Gladys, producing a handful of knotty, bruised fruit. "You see this? Now that wasn't just one hail. See, that goes to juice. When juice is $80 a ton, and that's what they're payin' now for a ton of apples, and you take your pick bill, your spray bill, your bill for handlin' and all the rest, that leaves the farmer with not but very little."

The Barnwells figure they'll have only about 30 percent of a crop.

"On the whole, Henderson County has a lot of apples, but we just got hit," says Odell. "Out here on the road, the hail didn't hit too bad. Around our house, it beat 'em up."

"We just don't have all that many apples," says Gladys. "We picked yesterday, and the same block we picked in one day yesterday took a week and a half last year. We got land that ain't been hit by hail up at the head of the creek, but it's not a big orchard. We're picking a few for the porch here, just trying to work with it the best we can."

"Course we had a lot of apples last year, but we didn't make no money," says Odell. "It's been three years since I made any money. Like an ol' feller told me a day or two ago, said he was comin' through Georgie, seen a sign that says, 'Let's legalize gambling. Why should the farmer have all the fun?'"

"Things have changed," says Gladys. "Apple prices haven't changed, but everything else has."

Things have changed a lot for the Barnwells, too.

Their families came to Henderson County from South Carolina to work in the orchards.

"I didn't get to go to school," says Odell, who has a droll sense of humor. "I just went one day in my sister's place."

"Don't listen to him," says Gladys. "He tells that to everybody."

Actually, both quit school at early ages.

"I wove rugs," says Gladys. "That's what I did when I quit school and went to work. We didn't get that big high school education like we give our young'uns.

Odell quit to work in the orchards, and after he and Gladys married, they, like their parents before them, moved into an orchard house and continued to work in apples, making as little as $2 a day. There they stayed 10 years, dreaming of better times.

"I never did like sharecropping," says Gladys. "All I ever thought about was having a roof over my head to call my own."

During that time, they managed to buy 15 acres of their own and set them out in apples. They tended to their own orchard after work and on weekends, and eventually they were able to get together enough money for a down payment on an old house, a roof of their own, and quit sharecropping.

Most of their crop they sold from the back of a truck on the Greenville highway. "We hung our babies on the side of the truck in a little car seat," Gladys recalls.

There were five babies altogether, one daughter and four sons, all grown now, all still in the apple business with their parents.

Hard work and prudence have given the Barnwells 80 scattered acres of orchards, plus a big brick packing house by the side of the highway on the edge of Hendersonville.

The accomplishment causes Odell to look back in wonder.

"You know, I'd of had it made if I'd got to go two days of school, wouldn't I?" he says, trying to hide a grin.

This summer, the packing house is largely idle. "We can't even pack an apple," Gladys says. What apples they do have, they are selling from the covered front of the packing house, the area they call the porch. From July until Christmas, either Odell or Gladys, or both, can be found there seven days a week, 8 a.m. until dark. And when they aren't busy selling apples, they're usually telling stories.

They tell the one about the time Odell was trying to figure up the price of some apples for a customer and got so tangled up that he just gave up and told her, "Lady, I went to night school and I just can't figure day time."

Odell doesn't like dealing with the public as much as Gladys does, and he can sometimes be impatient with a customer. A few days earlier, a woman in a new Cadillac with Florida license tags stopped and inquired about the price of apples. When Odell told her $7 a bushel, she said it was too high.

"She said, 'Lord have mercy, I'm retired, can't I get a discount?'" Odell recalls. "I said, lady, I'll be 65 June coming, and you know what I'm gonna do? I'm goina retire and get me a new car and go

174

down the road complaining just like you. That's what I told her. Then I just come back and sat down."

"I heard that," says Gladys, "and I said, 'Uh-oh, that's a sign he's been here too long.' But I'll tell you, the public's something else, feller."

"You don't know where a feller could find a good job, do you?" says Odell.

Passage

At Hendersonville, license tags and newspapers tell a story. Florida tags—most on big, expensive cars—seem to outnumber North Carolina tags on the town's streets. At the town's newsstand, more Florida than North Carolina newspapers are offered for sale.

The story is simple. Hendersonville is not just a North Carolina mountain town. It is a mecca for affluent Florida people.

Why Hendersonville?

Probably because it's one of the southernmost mountain towns conveniently on an interstate highway. At first the Florida people, most of whom originally were from the North, came seeking refuge from Florida's devastating summer heat. They stayed to buy land, build houses and spread in large numbers throughout the western-most part of the state, changing the mountains and their character forever.

On the western edge of Hendersonville, the highway passes Oakdale Cemetery, and from the road can be seen the marble angel that inspired Thomas Wolfe's famous novel, "Look Homeward, Angel." The angel, which graces the grave of Margaret Johnson, was seriously damaged by a tourist who toppled it in 1973. It has since been patched back together and fenced to protect it.

Five miles from Hendersonville, at Horse Shoe, a sign in front of Amanda's Antique Shop advertises the largest button collection in the South.

"We didn't know anything about buttons," says Margaret Bagwell, who bought the collection with her sister, Jane McSweeny, at an estate sale six months ago. The collection—more than a quarter of a million buttons in a myriad of shapes, sizes and materials—has since attracted attention from button collectors all over the country, including the author of "The Big Book of Buttons," the bible of button collectors.

The buttons, many of them rare and dating back more than 100 years, were collected over a lifetime by an elderly Florida woman who died last year. Jane and Margaret advertised the entire collection for sale at $20,000 before they realized its value was many times that. They are now classifying, carding and pricing the buttons individually, showing and selling them in their shop.

"How can you describe this many buttons?" says Jane, pulling out drawers stuffed with buttons. "You have to come and see it."

Etowah, three miles from Horse Shoe, offers a glimpse of what

176

will become a familiar sight along the next 50 miles of the highway: golf courses and condominiums.

Brevard, county seat of Transylvania County, home of Brevard College, announces itself even before the highway leaves Henderson County just west of Etowah. Foul smelling discharges from the Olin Corporation's plant in Brevard, which makes cigarette papers and fine papers for Bibles, waft eastward in early morning and late afternoon.

Transylvania County, with a 1980 population of fewer than 24,000, has been described as having more real estate agents per capita than any other county in the state, but 36 percent of its 379 square miles is owned by the federal government, most of it in Pisgah National Forest, America's first national forest. The highway skirts the forest for much of its passage through the county.

West of the intersection with U.S. 178, the highway begins to climb. For the next 60 miles, it is an old-time mountain road, ever ascending and descending, winding and cutting back on itself. Several miles after it begins its climb, the highway crosses the top of spectacular Toxaway Falls. To the south, the falls cascade down a wide granite trough carved by the river out of the side of Toxaway Mountain. To the north, an earthen dam looms high above the highway, holding back Lake Toxaway.

Lake Toxaway, a 540-acre lake built at century's turn, became a popular resort for America's super rich, who came up the mountain by train from South Carolina. But in 1916, after days of unrelenting rain that brought disastrous flooding throughout the mountains, the dam broke, the lake gushed down the mountain and the resort died. Trees grew in the lake bottom, but in 1961 developers rebuilt the dam and made the lake nearly twice as big as it was originally, 900 acres, the largest privately owned lake in the state. Lots were sold for expensive homes, and the lake is once again a popular resort for the well-to-do.

Condos and land sale offices abound along the highway as it passes on to Sapphire, a community of gift shops and country clubs, where a restaurant called Alfie's is featuring something other than mountain fare—an oyster festival, "raw, steamed, casino, Rockefeller."

West of Sapphire, the highway winds for five miles through a single resort development, Fairfield Sapphire Valley, a carefully planned and controlled community of condos, ski slopes, riding trails, golf courses, tennis and racquet ball courts built around the picturesque Fairfield Inn, which opened in 1896.

Beyond Cashiers, yet another resort town for the well-monied, the highway begins the climb up Cowee Mountain toward Highlands. At the Jackson-Macon county line, a spectacular view opens in the trees. In the foreground is the Devil's Courthouse, part of Whiteside

Mountain, which on its far side has sheer cliffs of 1,800 feet, highest cliffs east of the Rocky Mountains. In the distance are Chimney Top and Rock Mountains.

Highlands is a country club town, a town of old inns, art auctions, gourmet restaurants, boutiques, shops selling Irish linen, Waterford crystal and Wedgewood china. It is a town of Cadillacs and Mercedes and elegant homes hidden in the trees, marked only by huge stone gates at the foot of winding drives.

Once its welcoming signs noted that it was the highest town east of the Rockies, at 3,838 feet, but those signs had to come down when Beech Mountain in Avery County, elevation 5,505 feet, incorporated in 1981. That's one of the few things that Highlands can't legitimately boast about anymore.

Retirement Haven Number One

BREVARD   "Brevard Is Number One!" read the headline on the
front page of the Transylvania Times on Dec. 15, 1983.

The story was not about the local high school football team
winning a championship. It was something far more significant for
this mountain town, which could claim only 5,300 people in the
1980 census.

A new book, "Places Rated Retirement Guide," had just come out.
It had examined 107 cities and towns around America as potential
retirement spots, rating them on matters of primary concern to
retired folks: climate, housing, economics, crime, health care and
livability-recreation. Brevard had come out on top.

The news had broken the day before in USA Today. News services
had sent it to newspapers, radio and TV stations around the world.
Soon Brevard was being talked about on the Today Show and written
about in magazines. The response was immediate and is still
building.

"Oh, it's thousands and thousands," says Esther Wesley, taking
three legal pad sheets from the wall by her desk. On the sheets she
has been trying to keep track of letters that have come from every
state and 11 countries since Brevard was proclaimed America's best
retirement spot.

"Mainly from Florida," she says, "but we had a great deal of
correspondence from New York and New Jersey, Illinois, California,
Michigan, Ohio . . ."

Esther, who came to Brevard from New Jersey nine years ago, is
executive secretary of the Brevard Chamber of Commerce. Until
last December, she was the chamber's only employee. But a second
person had to be hired just to handle the mail brought by all the
attention Brevard received after its rating.

How many of the people who have written for information have
actually retired to Brevard so far Esther doesn't know, but she does
know that a lot of people have come to see the town for themselves.
She's certain that many will be back to live.

"Anybody who has ever traveled through Brevard has felt the
warmth of it," she says. "First the beauty catches their eye, and if
they stop anywhere, they're attracted to the friendliness, the
warmth. This is truly southern hospitality here."

Judging the effect of Brevard's rating might take years. Most people
about to retire check a lot of places before deciding where to spend
the last years of their lives, but at least two developers are counting

179

on large numbers of them deciding on Brevard.

"People were discovering this country before that rating came out," says Bob Frickhoeffer, pointing out that several developments near Brevard have already attracted large numbers of people retiring from other areas.

Bob, who came to Brevard from Charlotte three years ago, is marketing director for Carefree Carolina, a huge new retirement development getting started just off U.S. 64 in Brevard on the former site of Camp Carolina, a vintage boy's camp. The development will offer condominiums with prices beginning above $70,000 and restricted homesites. Negotiations are under way to include a large apartment complex with an infirmary, full-time medical care and a cafeteria. When completed, the development should have 700 homes.

"Our amenities are aimed toward an active lifestyle," Bob says. "We're talking racquetball courts, tennis courts, swimming pool, walking trails, jacuzzis, things to keep the retirees active, not just put 'em on the porch in a rocking chair."

So far, eight apartments have been built, 10 sold at Carefree Carolina, but no retirees have yet moved in. Things have been moving faster across town at Waterford Place, another new retirement development next to the Brevard Music Center. Waterford Place will have only 100 apartments and houses starting at about $75,000. So far 11 have been occupied and workmen are rushing to complete other units already sold.

Carole Merrill is the youngest person living at Waterford Place. She's 40. She's also sales agent for the development. In less that a year, she's sold 31 apartments and houses. Average age of buyers: 67. Most common profession: engineer. Means of payment: cash.

"We've had 13 states represented so far," she says, "the majority from New York, Michigan, and then we're having the Florida back transfers: the people who have been in Florida five to seven years and are moving back this way because of heat and overpopulation.

"Where are you folks from?" she asks a couple being shown a model home by a real estate agent.

"We're from Wisconsin," says Robert Torbenson of Hudson.

Robert has been with the 3M Co. 23 years. Next year, he'll be 62 and eligible to retire. He and his wife, Helene, who have two daughters and four grandchildren in Wisconsin, can't wait to leave their home state.

"Have you ever been there in winter?" asks Helene, explaining why.

"We had snowbanks in front of our house last year as high as this ceiling," Robert says. "I've shoveled my share of snow over my lifetime."

For several years the Torbensons have used their vacations to investigate retirement spots. Previously, they'd looked only in Florida.

"I've seen enough of Florida," says Robert, who has firmly decided against moving there.

He and Helene were drawn to Brevard, which has an average of only five snow days a year, because of the "Places Rated Retirement Guide." This was their first day of looking.

"So far," says Robert, "we like it very much. We're more interested in a small town. We live in a small town now so we want to stay with one."

The influx of outsiders is changing Brevard, and some local people aren't sure what to think of it all.

"When you talk to my daddy, he calls 'em furriners," says Carole Merrill, who was born and grew up in Brevard, "but now that they're his daughter's bread and butter, he has to look at it in a different way."

For herself, Carole couldn't be happier about the influx. "I can remember when we had one paved road, one red light, one cop, one grocery store and because of the people coming here, I've had a better opportunity. I had a better education, a better opportunity for so many things. Being an optimist, I'll continue to feel that way until it proves otherwise, and so far it hasn't. That's the truth. That's not a sales pitch."

Helen Ronse will never forget the day she moved into her new retirement home a few miles outside Brevard. That evening the doorbell rang and at the door stood the young local woman from next door, holding a tray.

"She said, 'You're the first northerner that I've talked to,'" Helen says, laughing at the memory, "so I asked my husband what do northerners eat and he said chicken pie."

On the tray was a freshly baked chicken pie, salad, cherry cobbler and homemade bread.

"We laughed about that a lot together later," Helen says. "She's a good buddy now."

"She's a good cook, too," adds her husband, Julian.

"In all our other moves," says Helen, "I don't think I liked most of the people as immediately as I liked the people here. I think there's a special integrity here. I call it a code of the true natives. They were extremely helpful, extremely courteous, just a high degree of integrity."

Helen and Julian moved to Brevard from an exclusive suburb of Detroit. She was an executive with a chain of retail stores, he an engineer with AT&T. They moved a lot in their careers. In 1970, they bought a house in the Florida Keys with the idea of retiring there. But as they watched the area deteriorate, they began thinking of retiring somewhere else.

A friend told them about Lake Lure. They had heard about Hendersonville in Florida. Somebody else told them Franklin was nice, and in an earlier book about retirement to the Sun Belt they had read that "Brevard has everything." So on their way home from

181

a Florida trip in March 1979, they mapped out a side trip from Lake Lure, through Hendersonville and Brevard and on to Franklin.

The Ronses have lived in Brevard for four years now and have no regrets about their decision.

"It might be nice to go to the Loop in Chicago or Fifth Avenue in New York and shop up and down, but you don't need it," Helen says.

She and Julian are very active in the Transylvania Chapter of the American Association of Retired Persons, the largest chapter in western North Carolina with 576 members. Helen is now president of the group, which meets monthly, conducts regular activities for members, sponsors cultural events for the community, and provides volunteers for the hospital, the hospice, nursing homes, meals on wheels and almost every fund-raising event in the area.

Helen and Julian have made only one change since their retirement. After nearly four years living outside of town, they decided they'd rather live in Brevard. So they sold the first house they bought and built a new one. They have just moved in. Furniture is not yet arranged and workmen are still putting on finishing touches as Helen talks about her fondness for Brevard.

"We decided this is the last, absolute, ever-loving move that we ever make in our lives," she says.

Mountain Man

QUEBEC   Just up the road from Woodrow Fisher's little house by the side of U.S. 64, racquetball courts are being built. A gift shop has opened practically next door. Condominiums rise on mountain sides all around. Not far from his house, small lots on land once considered worthless go for $12,000 and more. In hollows where he once hunted and trapped, golfers stride in flashy clothes.

Woodrow shakes his head in wonder at it all.

"You go out from here now, and you don't even know where you are hardly," he says, wheezing as he talks.

Woodrow doesn't get out much anymore.

"I can't," he says. "I got emphysema. It's fouled my breathing up. I just ain't got the breath to do much. I would like to get out and fish some, but I can't. Sometimes, huntin' season, my brother'll come. We'll ride around, kill a few squirrels from the road in his pickup."

Woodrow will soon be 72. He wears overalls because that's what mountain men have traditionally worn. He was born in this community near Lake Toxaway. His roots go deep.

"My father and my mother, my grandfather and grandmother; they was all raised here."

His father, who worked maintaining the railroad spur that came up Toxaway Mountain, had 49 acres on which his family was self-sufficient when Woodrow was growing up. They grew corn, potatoes, vegetables, raised hogs, kept a milk cow. They hunted and trapped and fished.

Woodrow, who only got to the eighth grade in school, learned to trap as a boy, and as a young man he made his living trapping and timbering. Few jobs were to be had. The only industry nearby, besides sawmills, was the tannery at Rosman. Young people looking for work often went off to the cotton mills in South Carolina, and Woodrow tried that briefly. But he didn't like it and returned to the hills. Money could be made in other ways.

"Well, there was a lot of whiskey made," says Woodrow, who made a considerable amount himself back in the '30s.

"Got caught once," he says. "Right across the hill about two miles from here. Give me a suspended sentence. I never did serve no time. We come back and picked up them barrels and set back up after they cut 'em down."

"In this area here there wasn't but one family that didn't have something to do with it for miles and miles," says Woodrow's wife, Effie, whose daddy was a moonshiner.

Woodrow wasn't only good at making whiskey, he was good at drinking it.

"Yeah, I drank some," he says.

"I'd say a good bit," Effie says.

"I guess a drink wouldn't hurt a man," says Woodrow, "but I'd usually drink too much if I got ahold of it."

I'll second that," Effie says.

"I got a gallon about a year or so ago, I drank about half of it," Woodrow says, "It made me purty sick and I sold the other half."

"Yeah," says Effie, "but you got a gallon, too, that you set here and drank it right up.

"Made him so sick I had to sit up with him day and night."

Woodrow grins.

"They don't make it like they used to," he says.

Near the end of the Depression, Woodrow managed to get a job at the paper mill that had opened in Brevard. Then he got drafted into the army when World War II started. He got sent off to the Arctic Circle, and when he came home on leave in 1943, just before being shipped to Utah, he married Effie.

After the war, he went back to the paper mill and Effie saw to it that he didn't make any more liquor. In 1948, they bought the little house where they live and six acres for $1,800. Over the years, they fixed up the house, added a basement, made it snug and comfortable. Here, they reared their four children—three daughters and a son.

Woodrow has been retired seven years now. He and Effie have three grandchildren. Their three married daughters all live close by. Their unmarried son lives with them. And all feel a little like strangers in their own land.

They are surrounded by outsiders, wealthy people from Florida and other places who came and bought land and developed it, attracting more and more outsiders, driving land prices higher and higher, changing everything.

"I guess it's all right for the people that's a'doin' it," says Woodrow, "but it's about destroyed these mountains. Used to be you could go anywhere you wanted to and hunt and nobody said anything to you about it. Now if you step off the road, you're on somebody's property and somebody's squawking at you."

"It's hard on young people around here," Effie says. "They don't have anywhere to fish or hunt. Children now growing up don't have anything like that at all. No wonder they're getting into stuff."

"People around here's not too fond of what's happening," says Woodrow, "but I don't think there's nothin' you can do about it if you believe in private ownership."

Behind their house is a small shell of a cabin on a small piece of land. It has been sold to a succession of Florida people, most recently about three years ago.

"I could've bought it for $2,700 one time, and it sold the last time for $29,000," Woodrow says.

Effie worries that her children and grandchildren won't be able to stay in the mountains that their ancestors settled. "They fix it so us people can't afford the land," she says. "Our children just can't afford to pay the price. That's why we stick to this place. We want to give it to the children."

Woodrow can't remember all the times Florida people have tried to get him to sell his house and land. He's always polite with them, but he always tells them the same thing: no, thank you.

"This one Florida woman come back and she tried to buy this place from me," Effie says. "She said, 'Do you want to sell your place?' and I said, 'It's our home,' and she said, 'I didn't ask you that, I asked you do you want to sell it,' and I just said, 'No, ma'am, I don't.'"

The Painter in the Church

CASHIERS Drawn by the ghosts of ancestors, William Whiteside, a painter known to friends as Bill, first came to the mountains in 1968.

"When I drove into this area, I felt more at home here than I did in Florida where I was born," he says. "Something about it that satisfied something deep inside. Well, maybe it's something in the memory cells."

He had come that summer at the behest of an aunt who wanted him to see the graves of his great-grandfather and great-great-grandfather. His great-great-grandfather was one of the first settlers in the Hickory Nut Gorge. He carved out a big plantation along the Rocky Broad River, a plantation later covered by the waters of Lake Lure. His great-grandfather raised horses for Confederate General Wade Hampton, who had a home near Cashiers. Another ancestor surveyed vast areas of the mountains.

Bill's great-grandfather was first in the family to make a Florida connection. He is believed to be the first North Carolinian to drive to Florida for a winter vacation, driving a wagon and team down and back, two months each way.

Bill's grandfather, a dairyman, was first in the family to leave the mountains, settling near Atlanta. His father, also a dairyman, moved to Bradenton, Fla., where Bill was born.

Bill's childhood was not easy.

"My father was an alcoholic," he says. "I stayed in the woods a lot with the animals and the cows. Things were pretty rough at home. I'd go sit in the woods with the rabbits and the quail and everything and just make friends with them."

Thinking about it now, he thinks that may be where the artistic spark in him was first ignited, but he can't be sure.

"I don't know where it came from," he says. "Some souls just come here sensitive."

Bill joined the Marines after high school and became a flight engineer on B-25s for more than 50 World War II combat missions in the South Pacific, where he won half a dozen medals. After the war, he enrolled at Georgia Tech to study aeronautical engineering. In his third year, he was poisoned by DDT in the milk served in the school cafeteria and had to return home to Florida to recuperate. While recovering, he began painting and took some courses at the

186

Ringling School of Art in Sarasota. He never went back to aeronautical engineering.

After three years at Ringling, he took a job as a commercial artist, a job that gave him frustration and ulcers until he enrolled at Florida State University in Tallahassee and got a degree in art education.

For three years, he taught art in public schools in Florida, then returned to Florida State to get a master's degree in painting. He taught at the school for a year before taking a job teaching painting at North Texas State University in Denton.

In 1968, the year he first came to see the mountains from which his family had sprung, Bill and his wife Esther, who had three children, made two big decisions. Bill gave up the security of teaching to see if he could make it as a painter. And he began looking for some way to come to live in the mountains where he felt so much at home.

From 1969 through 1972, while he was establishing himself as a painter, he brought his family to Cashiers every summer while he was artist in residence at High Hampton Inn. In 1973, he started teaching summer school at Western Carolina University at Cullowhee so they could continue coming to the mountains.

In 1974, Cashiers Baptist Church, which had built a new sanctuary, put its old church up for sale on the condition that the buyer move it. Bill bought it and six acres on U.S. 64 on which to put it before being told by three different house-moving companies that the church couldn't be moved. He worried about it for weeks before deciding to try to move it himself.

"I took a chain saw and cut it up in seven different pieces and got a big crane and loaded it on a truck and moved it up here. Then I put it back together. I did all the plumbing, wiring, block laying and everything."

The first winter, Bill and his family shivered in the old church while he built living quarters onto the back of it, quarters with room for painting and big windows for light and the view of Whiteside Mountain, which Bill believes was named for one of his ancestors. By the next summer, he was able to open the church as a gallery for his work.

Since then, Bill and the gallery have found great success. He sells his paintings—mostly landscapes in watercolors, acrylics and egg tempera, many of mountain scenes—as quickly as he produces them at prices up to $6,000. Burt Reynolds, who has a summer home nearby, bought some of his paintings and commissioned him to do a portrait of him in a scene from his movie, "Deliverance," which Bill is now finishing.

But now, after finding a home and success in the mountains, Bill and Esther are thinking about leaving.

"I don't know. I've reached another plateau in my life, and we feel like we've got to make a decision," Bill says as a chicken wanders into the gallery through the open front door. "Get out of here, chicken!

Get! Get!."

The chicken scurries out.

"She had about 10 little biddies in here one day," he says. "All those little biddy droppings weren't bad, but where the mother hen dropped was something else."

Life has changed dramatically for Bill and Esther in 10 years. In his work, although he has found success, Bill, who is now 59, has grown less productive and less content.

"Earlier, my taste was equal to my ability, and I was happy with almost everything I did," he says. "Now my taste is above my ability so I'm not satisfied with most of the things I do."

But it is in their family life that the greatest changes have occurred. In 1978, their eldest child, Albert, a brilliant young man with great promise, was killed when his car left a curve on a mountain road and pinned him underwater in a stream. They still grieve for him. Their other children, Norman, 26, and Susan, 23, have left home. Norman is in Miami, Susan in Atlanta.

"We've always been a close family," Bill says. "For 25 years, we had a very small world. We didn't need any friends much. All of a sudden now our children are gone. We're sitting up here in the winter looking at each other. I think since we lost Albert that the family has had to lean on each other a little more. The kids are closer now. We would like to spend more time with them. We're just having a hard time turning the kids loose. I might be a little too dependent on them."

He and Esther, who is away because her mother is ailing in Florida, are thinking about finding a place somewhere in northern Florida where they would be halfway between their children so that all of them could get together more.

"Right now, we're open to a change if something develops," Bill says. "But if we sell this place, we'll probably get a small house or something in the area so we can come back and keep in touch."

He looks up to see the chicken sneaking back in the front door.

"Chicken, go on! Get out of here!"

The Biggest House in Town

HIGHLANDS   Not quite two years ago, Glenn and Shan Arnette, then newlyweds, decided what they needed was a house in the mountains.

They already had a winter house in exclusive Winter Park, Fla. They were planning a beachfront house back home in South Carolina for spring and fall. But they needed a place to escape the summer heat.

Highlands, they decided, was just the spot. It was a very nice little town, a summer town for those whose tastes for the finer things equal their ability to buy them. It had just the right ambiance.

Real estate agents were showing them around.

"They said, 'what do you want?'" Glenn remembers, "and I said, 'Something like that,'" and I pointed to the inn.

The Highlands Inn was opened in 1880, four years after Highlands was founded by two northern developers as a resort town for the very rich. Built by Joseph Halleck of virgin timber and handmade nails, the inn was three stories tall, had more than 30 guest rooms and a double-decker porch across the front. Opened as the Highlands House, it became Smith Hotel three years later when it was bought by John J. Smith. It became Highlands Inn during the Depression when Frank Cook bought it. Helen Major took it over in the '60s and operated it for 10 years before selling it to a Florida resident, Rye Page.

When Glenn pointed at the inn that day, one of the real estate agents said, "It might be for sale."

"We laughed about it and went back to Florida," Glenn says. "Next thing I knew we had bought the biggest house in town."

The inn was indeed for sale and when the real estate agent called to tell them, Glenn and Shan, who'd been married six months after 10 years of dating, began thinking seriously about it. Both had experience in tourism. Shan and her family own and operate Lakewood Camping Resorts at Myrtle Beach. Glenn, who's 44, was director of the Myrtle Beach Convention Center for six years before moving to Buffalo, N.Y., to open and operate that city's convention center. He was there until he married, and the couple saw the inn as a challenge.

"I love a challenge," Glenn says. "I wanted to take a piece of history and do something with it. We wanted to bring it back to life. The old girl was worn out when we bought her."

189

Highlands Inn

They bought the inn in 1983 and immediately began complete renovation. They painted it inside and out, installed new carpets and furnishings, added a show room, a private club with complete business news services, stock exchange wires and brokerage phones, an English tea room, roof garden and porch restaurants in addition to the traditional dining room with its solid cherry floors, then started a new addition on the back with 12 guest rooms and a card room.

"What we've done," says Glenn, "is restore the inn to its elegance. We are the oldest inn in this area but we are not like any other inn around here. We are not country or whatever. We are strictly a New England-type inn."

After they finished refurbishing the inn, Glenn and Shan found the house in Highlands they were looking for, the old Bascom Estate, with 13 acres and a six-bedroom, five-and-a-half-bath house, which they have now renovated and made their summer home.

"We like to redo things," Glenn says. "Probably the best challenge we ever had was to take the inn and redo it and make it work again for the people of Highlands. People here are very particular. Highlands is a wealthy second-home community, a *very* wealthy second-home community. The shops are quality, the attitude is good. People don't want to destroy that. They don't want Hardee's and McDonald's and things like that. I think at first they were afraid of what we were going to do. However, we've given their history back to them. We don't even think of ourselves as owning the inn. We're really just taking care of the inn for a time."

The rejuvenation has brought more business than ever to the inn. The musical revue that Glenn started in the show room this summer has been sold out every night with a 10-day waiting list.

"Our clientele?" Glenn asks. "Oh, it's Palm Beach, Fort Lauderdale, Savannah, Charleston, New Orleans. That's basically it."

In midweek, during the lull between the summer rush and the fall-leaf rush, only two people are taking the evening air in the black rockers and wicker chairs amid the flower pots and hanging baskets on the front porch of the inn. They are Millie and Ted Bergman of Howey-in-the-Hills, Florida, 35 miles west of Orlando. Millie is wearing a knit coat, Ted a sweater, against the evening chill. Ted, who's 85, is smoking a pipe. Millie, who's discreet about her age, has blue hair.

"We hadn't been here in years," Ted says. "We used to come up pretty regularly 20 or 25 years ago."

"That was when the Cooks had it," Millie says.

Millie and Ted have been married 56 years. They have one daughter, three grandchildren, five great-grandchildren. Ted has been retired 12 years after working 47 years for Florida Power & Light Co.

"We got here today; we didn't know a soul," Ted says. They also were surprised but pleased with the changes in the inn. They took one of the more expensive rooms in the new wing.

"It's been a long time," Ted says. "We just decided we'd like to come back up here and enjoy this old hotel where we used to have so much fun. We made a lot of friends here in days gone by.

"There was an old widower from Charlotte we used to see up here. He loved to play gin rummy and we would play. He would have a cocktail party up in his room and invite some of the guests."

"He was so cute, so good-looking," Millie adds.

"His name was Mr. Jones," Ted says.

"He was from Georgia," Millie says.

"No, he was from Charlotte."

"I thought he was from Georgia. Well, anyway, he could tell some real good jokes."

"Loved to play gin rummy," Ted says.

"Real good jokes," Millie says.

Passage

Cullasaja, the Cherokees called the river. Sugar Water.

Where U.S. 64 first encounters it, the river is tamed into the mirror waters of Highlands Lake. Escaping over the stone dam by the highway west of Highlands, it begins its 18-mile run, wild and free, through a rugged gorge to Franklin, where it joins the Little Tennessee. The highway tries to tag along but the river goes to places it cannot follow, frequently leaving it high above, clinging precariously to the mountainsides.

This is the land of waterfalls. The first along the highway west of Highlands is Bridal Veil Falls, one of the most popular in the state. Here Mill Creek falls 120 feet off Rich Mountain before it joins the Cullasaja. Once the highway ran behind the waterfall under the overhang of the cliff but now it passes beside it. The old part of the road has been left, though, so that tourists still may drive under the falls. On this day, appropriately, newlyweds from Palm Beach, Fla., their small car still gaudy with the honeymoon graffiti of friends, takes a good-luck turn behind the falls, waving happily at other tourists taking snapshots.

West of Bridal Veil Falls, not visible from the highway, the Cullasaja drops 75 feet over a ledge, creating Dry Falls, so named because it is possible to walk behind the falls without getting wet. Further downstream, the river passes through a series of falls, dropping 310 feet in a quarter mile.

Here, the highway is old-style mountain road, twisting torturously, shoulderless and precarious, overhanging trees giving it a cavelike effect. Above the Lower Cullasaja Falls, it reaches the most harrowing point on its entire passage through the state, carved on blind curves into the mountainside. On one side, the stone face of the mountain rises almost perpendicular from the highway's edge. On the other side is a long drop over a sheer cliff with only a narrow stone wall, no more than a foot high, standing guard. Not the kind of place to take an eye off the road to catch a glimpse of the glorious scenery below.

Leaving the mountain, the river gorge and this section of Nantahala National Forest behind, the highway returns to summer homes and subdivisions, campgrounds, gift shops, trout farms, fruit stands and gem shops as it approaches Franklin, county seat of Macon County, a town with a population of 2,800 that swells 10 times in summer, mostly with Florida people.

On the eastern edge of Franklin, the highway joins U.S. highways

23 and 441 for a four-lane sweep past the town. Murphy is 54 miles away. For seven miles the highway, still four lanes, passes through valley with mountains on every horizon. Macon County has 27 peaks more than 4,000 feet high, 17 of them more than 5,000 feet.

At Cartoogechaye Creek, where Old 64 goes off on its winding and lonely path, the new highway becomes two lanes and begins to climb again. This is new-style mountain road, with wide shoulders, sturdy guard rails and no sharp curves, the kind that cares little for the ruggedness of mountains. New mountain roads simply bully their way through and over mountains, allowing traffic to flow without impediments.

Back into the Nantahala National Forest, back into wilderness the highway goes as it climbs, offering spectacular views. At Winding Stair Gap, elevation 3,820 feet, the highway has been blasted through the mountain top, leaving high-tiered cliffs of granite on each side of the road. The cliffs are water-stained, as if the mountain were weeping at the indignity of its wounds.

Purple and yellow wildflowers brighten the roadsides, and at September's end, the mountainsides are already tinged with premature autumn color brought by drought.

Where Old 64 cuts again into the highway, leading off to Wallace Gap, the Appalachian Trail crosses. To the south is Standing Indian Mountain, at 5,500 feet the highest peak in Macon County.

The highway is climbing again as it enters Clay County, smallest and least-populated county in the state with only 219 square miles of territory and 6,600 people.

Clay County has only one major highway, U.S. 64, and only one town, Hayesville, with about 500 people. There is not a full-fledged stoplight in the entire county.

As the highway tops Chunky Gal Mountain and begins its long descent back to valley, much of Clay County can be seen from an overlook where somebody has used a spray can to paint "God Bless the U.S.A." in big letters along the guard rail.

The first sign of civilization as the highway once again leaves the national forest is Neal Parker's small mountainside garage.

"I bought 73 acres up here before this new road come through," says Neal, who's 72. "Six months after I bought it they started surveying the road. I figured I might as well put something up here."

Shooting Creek, the first community in the valley, is farm country, and the odor from the chicken houses and hog lots proves it. West of Shooting Creek, condominiums appear as the highway skirts Chatuge Lake, a TVA lake on the Hiawassee River that backs up well into Georgia.

The lake is serene, green and peopleless on a weekday afternoon.

A by-pass carries the highway around Hayesville, but 64 Business still winds through the center of town. At the People's Store, an old-time general store on the square beside the courthouse, the town gathering place, owner Wayne Phillips, who admits to being in his 60s, has posted his operating hours on the door: "Open most days about 9 or 10, occasionally as early as 7, but some days as late as 12 or 1. We close about 5:30 or 6, occasionally about 4 or 5, but sometimes as late as 11 or 12. Some days or afternoons we aren't here at all and lately I've been here just about all the time except when I'm someplace else, but I should be here then, too."

Just inside the door sits a massive rocking chair, made of logs, big enough for several people.

"It's make of wormy chestnut, and it's got hemlock rockers," Wayne says. "You know, when a hemlock gets some age on it, it grows a crooked limb, and that's what the rockers are made of. I had it made when I had my first grandchild here a few years back because there wasn't a rocking chair in the house that was big enough for me."

Eight miles west of Hayesville, the highway crosses into Cherokee County and follows the wide and shallow Hiawassee River to Murphy, last town on its passage through the state.

Gemstone City

FRANKLIN   When Franklin makes the national news, as it does now and then, the story is invariably the same. Somebody, usually a tourist, has just found a huge ruby or star sapphire weighing hundreds of carats and valued at thousands of dollars.

People in Franklin love those stories. They know that such stories fire visions of quick and easy fortunes and keep the tourists coming.

Without question, gemstones bring the tourists to Franklin, and the town, which immodestly calls itself "the gem capital of the world," is well aware of it.

Some 10 different gems are found around Franklin, including rubies, sapphires, garnets, rhodolite, turquoise and amethyst, plus perhaps 30 different minerals valued by rockhounds. But it's the rubies and sapphires that are the big draw. Both are forms of corundum, crystals second in hardness only to diamonds. Red corundum is ruby. Other colors are sapphires. Corundum of many colors abounds in the Cowee Valley just off N.C. Highway 28 north of Franklin. It is the only ruby-producing area in America and one of only two places on earth (the other is in the Mogock Valley of Burma) where the famous deep red pigeon blood ruby, rarest of all rubies, is found.

Nobody knows who found the first rubies along Cowee Creek, probably Indians, but in 1893 reports of farmers finding such stones on their land prompted the Tiffany Co. of New York to send an expert to investigate. Dr. George Fredrick Knuz's report caused the company to buy hundreds of acres in the area and begin mining in 1895. Several deep shafts were sunk along the creek, but the source never was found, and after four years the company gave up. Later mining efforts likewise ended in failure.

For nearly half a century, the precious stones of Cowee Valley were largely ignored. Only local residents occasionally searched the creeks for them. Old-timers tell of using rubies and sapphires as slingshot ammunition when they were children.

But now and then outsiders would come, having heard tales of the fabulous stones in the area, and nearly 35 years ago one offered $5 to Weaver Gibson, a farmer on Caler branch of Cowee Creek, to let him look for stones on his land. Weaver laughed and accepted $1, all he thought it was worth. But later he and his brother, Carroll, got to thinking if one person was willing to pay to search for rocks, others might be, too. They opened the first ruby and sapphire mine for tourists on Weaver's farm in 1950. Within two years two other

195

Al and Marion Hall at museum

farmers opened mines nearby, and by the mid-'50s the Cowee mines were getting national attention in newspapers and magazines. The tourists have been coming ever since, from all over this country and other countries as well.

Now Franklin boasts nearly two dozen mines where tourists pay entrance fees, then buy buckets of mud and gravel to wash and sift in search of rubies, sapphires, garnets and other stones. Some of the mines salt the buckets with cheap polished stones from other areas. By law the mines must post notices if their gravel is "enriched."

"These tourists, they have to find something about every bucket or they go home mad," says Ernest Klatt, owner of Gem City Mine, explaining why his mine offers salted gravels.

In addition to the mines, Franklin has more than a dozen shops where gems and minerals are bought, sold, traded, cut, shaped, polished. And each year in July, the town holds a four-day "Gemboree," which attracted 8,000 people this summer. The Gem and Mineral Society, which has 175 members in Franklin, operates a gem and mineral museum in the old Macon County Jail in down-town Franklin (open May–Oct., 10-4 every day but Sunday 1-4).

"Let me show you something," says Al Hall, flipping off the lights in a small room of the museum.

Behind a glass, a wallful of rocks begins to glow in brilliant colors—orange, yellow, red, green, blue, purple.

"Isn't that fantastic? What you see is just the rocks. There is not a bit of paint in there. This is called our fluorescent room. We've been told it's the finest in the world, and people come from all over the world just to see this."

Al is the society's museum chairman. He and his wife, Marion, serve as hosts at the museum one day a week.

When Al and Marion retired from their hot dog stand in upstate New York, they moved to Key Largo in the Florida Keys and became shell collectors. Heat, crime and overpopulation caused them to move to Franklin two years ago, bringing their shells with them. Their museum-quality collection still remains in the five big crates it was moved in because the Halls are now rockhounds who spend at least three days a month searching for new treasures.

"When we moved here, I didn't know the difference between a ruby and a garnet," says Al. "Then we joined the gem society and just got deeper and deeper and deeper involved."

All it took for Al and Marion was one visit to the society's free museum, which they think should be the first stop for anybody coming to Franklin with gemstones in mind.

"I think a lot of people, once they see this museum, become collectors," says Al.

Not far away, Ernest Klatt, who's 72, operates his own free museum at his Ruby City Gems, the biggest gem and mineral shop in the Southeast, he says. Ernest is an Oklahoman who moved to Florida in 1932 and got rich in the real estate business.

197

"Made a lot of money," he says. "Spent it on rocks."

He became interested in rock collecting when he first came to Franklin on vacation in 1955 and visited the ruby mines. In 1957, he bought a motel and other real estate in Franklin, and the following year he opened a gem shop in Ft. Lauderdale. He moved the shop to Franklin in 1960. In addition to the shop and Gem City Mine, he owns 19 acres in downtown Franklin and 3,000 mineral leases in the west, including the only mine in the world that produces green garnets.

Over the years, Ernest has got thousands of people started as rockhounds and has helped hundreds to get into the business.

"It's a growing business, and I think it's going to continue to grow. We're living in a mineral generation. The mineral specimens themselves are probably the best collecting you can get into, the best investment you can make."

His museum includes not only specimens he has found but entire collections he has bought and traded for over the years.

"I buy some good stuff and pay good money for it," he says. "Some of this stuff does, you know, get expensive. You can print more money anytime you want to, but you can't print no petrified dinosaur bones like these."

Ernest's museum has many things just as unusual as petrified dinosaur bones, including a fossilized sea creature as yet to be identified, red emeralds and a sapphire than weighs 385 pounds.

"An old Indian brought that in here about 14 years ago," Ernest says of the huge sapphire. "I think he brought it the day he dug it up. It had another 80-pound piece on the back that was broke off of it. He gave that to some guys to help him load it."

Ernest won't say what he paid for the huge stone.

"I just paid him what he asked for it. It wasn't very much considering what he had. Sometimes you get a bargain, sometimes you have to pay extra. I always figure minerals and rocks are more important than money. You only need money to buy groceries."

New Life Farm

HAYESVILLE   The farm is named New Life, and the mailbox by the side of the highway is festooned with a big blue ribbon tied into a bow.

"Come on in," says Steve Smith, thin, redhaired and bearded. "I'll show you our newest new life."

On a bed in a back room lies Paul, one day old, sleeping peacefully.

"That makes five of our own," Steve says, smiling at the baby.

In addition to Paul are Peter, 3, Matthew, 5, Kristie, 7, Katie, 9. Then there is Jennifer, 19. She is family, too, just as nearly four dozen other teenagers have been in the last nine years.

Steve and his wife, Mary, grew up in Rochester, N.Y., in happy, middle-class families. After their marriage, they moved to Palm Beach, Fla., where Steve was executive director for the Society for the Prevention of Blindness.

They were blessedly happy as they began their own family, but they knew that many people were not.

"We started seeing a lot of teenagers, primarily girls, pregnant, abused, addicted to drugs and alcohol," Steve says. "We're spirit-filled Christians. We just felt abundantly wealthy with good health and good living, and we just felt the love of the Lord and wanted to share it."

Steve and Mary decided to start taking troubled teenagers into their home, giving them love and a stable life, hoping to help get their lives on track. But not in Florida and not in the city. They felt a rural environment would be best—a farm.

Through Christian friends, they found a 68-acre farm that they could get rent-free in the mountains of North Carolina, at Crumpler, north of Jefferson, near the Virginia line. And in 1975 they moved there with the idea of becoming farmers.

"Three weeks later, we got our first girl," Steve says. "She was a real case—drug addict, alcoholic, schizophrenic, suicidal, prostitute."

Within two years, there had been several other girls for different periods, and Steve and Mary, who were trying to raise hogs, chickens and cattle without experience, were broke and in debt.

Friends helped them find a smaller place they could rent, just five acres, with two small houses on U.S. 64 east of Hayesville, still in the mountains but far from Crumpler. One of the houses had been remodeled, and the attic had been made into a dormitory space. It

Top step—Steve Smith (holding newborn son Paul) and wife Mary
Middle step (left to right)—Kristi, Jennifer, Peter and Matthew
Bottom step—Katie

would fit their needs, and it would give them land enough to try to be self-sufficient.

Bitter experience had taught them to scale down their dreams. They would keep goats for milk, raise rabbits for meat and a little extra income, grow a big garden. One of the girls they had taken in, Debbie, decided the new farm needed a name.

"She said because she had found a new life, she thought that would be a good name," Steve recalls.

It was a new life for everybody in the family. Steve went back to college at Western Carolina in Cullowhee and got a degree in education. He got a job teaching in Hiawassee, Ga., 12 miles away, and used his free time to get his small farm operating efficiently.

Now he keeps a small herd of goats, two dozen chickens, a calf, a pig, two dozen breeding rabbits, and each summer raises a big garden. This provides all the family's milk, eggs, meat and vegetables, plus a small income from surplus sales. Three years ago, he started raising minnows in a small pond and worms under his rabbit pens to sell to fishermen at nearby Lake Chatuge, providing extra income that has increased every year. After renting for five years, he and Mary were able to buy the small farm two years ago and now rent the smaller house.

As their own family has grown, they have had less room for taking in troubled teenagers. Until last year, there were three. Now there is only Jennifer.

"We've never said 'no' to anybody," Steve says. "We've just not had as many requests in the last few years. Maybe the good Lord thinks we need to slow down."

The most they had at one time was eight. Some stayed only a few months, one for six years. They came from many sources and many places.

"We never had to look for children," Steve says. "They just seemed to find us. They've come from Washington, D.C., Puerto Rico, Miami, New York, all over the place."

Sometimes they caused problems. One girl ran away and kept calling and threatening their lives. One of the two boys they took in stole the family van, which had no insurance and wasn't paid for, got drunk and totaled it.

"Patience," Steve says. "That's one of the things I just continually pray for."

Yet he and Mary have no regrets and no plans to stop taking in teenagers who need them, for there have been rewards as well.

"Within three miles," Steve says, "there are two girls that are now married, living with their husbands. One of them has a year-old baby. She's very happy. Two or three others are living in the community on their own. They come by and call up. One girl calls every morning."

Steve is certain that he and Mary have found their purpose and their place on five mountain acres called New Life Farm beside highway 64, and he can't imagine ever leaving it.

"It's just a great feeling to go out there and sit on the porch swing and smell the fresh split oak for the fire. Yesterday, I baled hay, got more than enough of that for the winter. I go into the canning room and see all the food put up for the winter. And how could I ask for more beautiful scenery? Why would I want to be anywhere else?"

Homer Frisby

HAYESVILLE   Homer Frisby was ignoring the phone again. He was out in the yard picking up chestnuts and let it ring. He figured it was just the widder anyway. That woman would aggravate a man to death.

"Every time I step out the door the phone rings and I have to come answer it, and she says, 'Where you been?'" he says with a snort. "I've never called her up only one time a-practicin' on it. I don't call nobody."

If it had been up to him, he'd never have had a dadburn phone to begin with. He had no more use for it than a coon dog does for a banjo. "Why, Lord no, I wouldn't give you a dime fer it. I wish he hadn't sent it here. I don't want to set here a-listenin' for the phone to ring. Law, law."

It was his stepgrandson, Ronnie, who insisted that he have it and paid for it. Homer finally agreed to it just to make him feel better. Same with the TV in the front room that Homer never watches. Ronnie sent that, too. Lately, he had even mentioned something about an indoor bathroom. That was where Homer was going to draw the line.

"Don't want one indoors," he said adamantly. "I've seen too many freeze and bust."

After all, he'd made it 89 years without one and he figured he could make it the rest of the way.

Homer was born in the mountains of Tennessee, but his family moved across the line into Graham County when he was a teenager and that's where he spent most of his life. A life of hard labor, Homer's has been. He worked on the railroad, farmed, held other jobs, made a little moonshine likker now and then. He had some lean years, but he got by. About 24 years ago, he up and left Graham County and bought seven acres and a small tin-roofed house with a vine-shaded porch in Clay County.

"They didn't run me off, but I don't know why I come over here," he says.

It's not easy finding his house. From Hayesville, the county seat, you head north out Tusquittee Road until you come to Greasy Creek Road, which isn't paved. Follow that a ways until you come to some ruts that lead off up into a hollow. When those ruts fork, you swing to the left, ford the creek, and there's Homer's place.

If the weather is pleasant, Homer likes to entertain visitors on the porch, where hunting dogs loll and hens nest in boxes on the rail.

Homer Frisby

"I just been married three times that I remember of," Homer says, taking his ease in a sturdy porch swing. "My third wife died 18 days after I moved here."

It was his third wife's daughter who gave birth to Ronnie, a sickly child born blind. "That was the pitifulest lookin' human I ever seen in my life to live," Homer says. He and his wife kept the boy a lot in his first year, and took him in permanently when he was a year old.

"Me and that ol' boy, I carried him many miles before his feet ever hit the ground," Homer says. "When he got big enough to walk, every time I'd come in, me so tired I couldn't hardly move, he'd take my hand and say, 'Let's go sommers.' Well, we'd go. He was like me. He couldn't stay still."

When he was old enough to go to school, Ronnie went off to the School for the Blind in Raleigh, where a talent for music began to show itself. Homer knew it was there.

"When he was just a little thing, he used to git up under the house—I had two ol' metal barrels under there—he'd git up under there, git a stick of stove wood in each hand and sing as loud as he could a-beatin' on them barrels a-makin' music."

Ronnie Milsap is still making music, now a big country music star. He has a mansion and a big ranch near Nashville.

"I don't know about last year, but the year before that, I think it was, he just made seven million," Homer says with a grin, "and I told him I don't see why he wants to fool around for that small amount."

Homer likes home just fine, doesn't care much for going anywhere, but he has been out to see Ronnie in his mansion, and he'll go to see him if he's performing within a reasonable range, say Asheville, Knoxville, Chattanooga, Atlanta, Greenville. Homer doesn't have to say a thing for Ronnie to know that he's there. One touch is all it takes.

"Out in Knoxville, he didn't know I was comin'. I slipped up to him. He was talkin' to a bunch of people. I touched him with my finger, and he said, 'Lordy mercy, Homer, what you a'doin' here?'"

Homer can't remember the last time that Ronnie came to see him. It's been a while, but Homer understands.

"Last time I went to see him, him and his wife claimed they'd be up here before cold weather set in, but I don't believe it till I see him a-comin'."

Homer's life now suits him fine. "I feel so good," he says. "I don't do nothin' much only set here and read and dip my snuff."

He takes out a tin of snuff and packs his lip full. "I don't know how many years I been a-usin' it," he says. "Up in the 70s, I reckon. Hit'll kill you, feller. I alas heered it would. I tell you, in 19 and 19, I worked with a ol' feller, he was 'bout dead with TB, and he couldn't spit off his bib. That snuff killed him, fer it got all over him. When a feller loses his teeth, he can't keep his snuff with him, you know."

Homer spends most of his time alone. A neighbor, Agnes Hamilton, comes up the hollow to check on him most days, often bringing food, as she has done this day. And then, of course, there's the widder, always calling.

"Called 15 or 20 times today," Homer says. "Oh Lord, she calls too much."

The widder lives about a mile away and has a nice farm. Homer admits that he has walked over to visit with her.

"I used to," he says, "but I've slowed up. She's a purty good lookin' woman in a way—if she wasn't so old. She's 62."

The Folk School

BRASSTOWN   Maple limbs blazed under the old black pot suspended from a tripod. Lucy Hyatt, wearing a long dress, apron, sturdy black shoes and a blue flowered bonnet, used a wooden paddle to stir the swelling corn kernels boiling in the pot.

"I see you got here in hominy time," she said to a smiling woman approaching the fire.

"Oh, it's looking good," the woman said. "We brought our own jar so we'd be sure we got some."

Aunt Lucy, as many call her, had started this pot of hominy five hours earlier with the help of her nephew, Charles Smith, a pharmacist clad in patched overalls, and his wife, Mary Jo, also wearing a long dress and bonnet, who were visiting from Toccoa, Ga.

First, they strained water through wood ashes to get a lye solution. They put the solution in the big pot and got a fire going under it. They added shelled field corn and boiled it for about an hour and a half until the husks began to come off. They poured off the lye solution and rinsed and scrubbed the corn until all the kernels were separated from their husks. Then they returned the corn to the pot to boil some more.

"How long does it take?" an onlooker asked Aunt Lucy.

"All day long. You start it of a mornin' and you end up at night. This has got a spell to go yet."

Around the fire, talk turned to eating hominy. Is it better with melted butter or bacon grease? Fry it with crumbled sausage, somebody said. Best way in the world to eat it. Aunt Lucy said she liked it fried in pork chop and ham drippings. Somebody asked how long she'd been making hominy.

"Oh, I've been making hominy all my life. My mother made hominy, so I learned from her. We make it at home sometimes."

But not often.

Aunt Lucy, who doesn't like to give her age (she's in her 80s, says her nephew) is a retired teacher (first and second grades) who mostly makes hominy now to demonstrate old mountain ways at the annual fall festival at John C. Campbell Folk School. The festival, held the first weekend in October, is the year's big event at the school, which is the only school of its kind in America.

John Campbell was an educator who traveled widely in the Appalachians. He thought the mountain people had been failed by their educational systems, and he dreamed of doing something to help them. He died in 1919 without realizing that dream, but his

Winthrop and Maebelle Withrow

wife, Olive, vowed to carry it on. In 1922, she and a friend, Marguerite Butler, went to Europe to study educational programs and became intrigued with the "folk high schools" of Denmark which tried to prepare young people to have rich and full lives in their home communities.

Olive and Marguerite decided to try to transplant that concept to the Appalachians. After a long search for an appropriate place to try their idea, they settled on a beautiful valley at Brasstown, a community in Clay County near the Cherokee County line on a road that seven years later would become U.S. 64 (now old 64). They chose Brasstown—which was so named because early settlers confused two Cherokee words, one meaning green place and the other brass—primarily because local people showed so much interest in the idea.

They opened their school in 1925 with 25 acres of donated land, an old farm house and a handful of students whom they tried to teach craft skills, more efficient farming methods, better uses of resources and pride in their culture.

Olive Campbell was a go-getter who couldn't abide idleness and within a year, she even had organized the idlers at Scroggs Store into productive activity. Some of the men would spend much of the day at the store talking and whittling on sticks with their pocket knives. Olive got them to carve animal figures as they sat and talked and she began building a market for their work. The idlers became the core of the Brasstown Carvers, whose work is now known and sold throughout the country. Most of the carvers are now women.

Like the mountains themselves, the school has changed much since its beginnings. Olive Campbell and Marguerite Butler remained active at the school until shortly before their deaths. Olive died in 1954, Marguerite in 1982. The school, a non-profit institution controlled by a board of directors, has seven staff members and uses a network of craftsmen who have settled in the area as part-time instructors. It has grown to 365 acres and a complex of buildings.

Mountain skills and crafts are still taught. Each year some 1,300 students attend weekend workshops, one- and two-week courses and extended work-study programs in woodworking, carving, blacksmithing, pottery making, spinning, weaving, quilting, basket making, homesteading, music making, folk dancing. But mountain people are rarely the students anymore.

"People from all over the country are coming here now," says Tom DeTitta, a former newspaper reporter now the school's public relations director, "but the school has maintained and is very concerned with its commitment to the local people."

"Our purpose is to enliven and enrich the lives of local people," says crafts co-ordinator Gladys Rogers, who has been with the school 11 years. "Now we're enlivening and enriching the lives of a lot of people from other places. But the local people, they always come first."

Local people, students and visitors from afar gather each Saturday night for the dances that have been a tradition at the school for more than half a century, but the big event that brings them together each year is the two-day fall festival.

Dozens of craftsmen display their wares and demonstrate their techniques. String bands play and sing, and buck dancers, cloggers and garland dancers perform. Local people such as Lucy Hyatt come to demonstrate how to split shingles, cook in Dutch ovens, spin and weave, churn and make soap, hominy, lard and cracklins, cider, ox yokes and many other things crucial to life in the mountains in earlier days.

Maebelle and Winthrup Withrow had seen all those things done before, had done most of them themselves growing up in the mountains, so they contented themselves on a porch making music with anybody who wanted to join in for anybody who wanted to listen. Maebelle on the banjo, Winthrup on guitar. A female fiddler sat in for a while, then the blacksmith abandoned his forge and came over with his mandolin.

"We're from Copper Hill, Tennessee," Maebelle said between tunes, "but we're North Carolina people. We was borned and raised in Cherokee County."

Maebelle and Winthrup, a retired mine employee, have been making music together since their marriage 45 years ago. Most of that time, Maebelle also played guitar, an instrument she learned as a child.

"About five years ago, he took me off guitar and put me on a banjer," Maebelle said, nodding at Winthrow. "I didn't think it was fair, but now I enjoy it. I'm not like nobody else a-playin' it, fer I just took it up myself.

"Me and him used to play on the radio at Copper Hill. We mostly play in the kitchen at home now. Bunch comes 'ever Sa'rday night and we just play and have a big time. We like to come over here just 'cause we enjoy it. We just come up and enjoy the crowd."

Frontier Town

MURPHY   The midmorning coffee drinkers are just beginning to filter into Betty Culberson's Country Kitchen, a narrow, aging restaurant next to the shoe shop on Tennessee Street in downtown Murphy.

Wynn Harding, wearing cowboy boots with his jeans, is telling a long and loud story about this ol' gal who picked him up at the Turtletown Tavern, just across the line in Tennessee. If you live in Murphy and want to go out and drink a beer, you have to go to Tennessee. Anyway, this ol' gal picked him up and took him home with her, up on one of these mountains, then tried to kill him. Fired three shots at him through the front door. Scared him so bad, he wrecked his pickup trying to get away.

"You take a good lookin' woman, and her mean, too, she'll deceive you," Wynn says. "They're worse than 10 bad men."

"You ain't tellin' me a damn thing about it," says a grinning man in his 70s wearing a camouflage hunting cap who identifies himself only as Walt. "I went through all that every weekend."

Wynn is 57. He grew up near Murphy but had to leave as a young man to find work. "When I left, there wasn't anything here, only just Brumby's little textile mill and Lee Shield's lumber yard."

He went to Ohio where he worked 30 years in a steel mill before being permanently laid off three years ago. Twice married and divorced, he decided to return home and reclaim his family's deteriorating old homeplace.

Walt spent half his life in Blairsville, Ga., just across the state line, but moved to Murphy in 1948. "Just took a notion I wanted Murphy for a while," he says.

"When I was a boy I used to come with my daddy over here in an ol' ox wagon, and the streets wasn't nothin' but a mudhole in the wintertime," he says. "you know where the ice plant is on the other side of the river? Ol' steer's belly would drag coming through the mud there. We'd make about two or three trips, bring rye, corn and wheat and sell it, and take fertilizer back to Blairsville."

Conversation drifts back to the days when you could still get a beer in Murphy, when the police had a place everybody called the bullpen for locking up the rowdies.

"How many beer joints used to be in this town?" somebody asks.

"Back when TVA was here? Lord, I don't know."

"There was one out on 64 they called the Bloody Bucket."

"It's changed a lot," somebody observes.

"It's a good town. It's just some of the people that's not so hot."

"Some of the old families still trying to strangle it."

"Some of our straight-laced Baptists trying to stop everything. They don't want anybody to have any fun."

"Wilder'n hell, that's what it was," says Walt with a grin of fond remembrance.

"You're in the wild west out here," says Charlie Guthrie.

Charlie doesn't live in Murphy. He just works here. Come December, he will have been editor of the Cherokee Scout, Murphy's twice-weekly newspaper, for three years. He lives in Hiawassee, Ga., 25 miles away, where he is also editor of that town's weekly. Both are published by the same newspaper chain.

Charlie is 46, a native of Alabama who has spent most of his career working for big-city papers in Florida. For 16 years, he had been coming to the mountains on vacation, and finally he decided to give up his job as state editor of the Orlando Sentinel for a new, simpler and lower paying life in the hills.

"I came up here to take it easy, the old country editor bit," says a harried Charlie, smoking a cigarette and fingering a coffee mug that advertises motor oil. "But, oh, God, it's unreal. I could put out a daily here, there's so much news going on. My mind is boggled. I thought I'd seen it all in 22 years in the business.

"I've always been basically a hard newsman. I only know how to do the job one way and that's report the news. I'm heavy into government news and it just hasn't been done that way here before. Not many public officials like me or agree with what I write. There've been attempts to get me fired. There are a lot of people who are really vicious.

"The basic truth is that politics permeates the social fabric here like I've never seen before. It's an anything-goes politics, the old school. Vote buying is traditional. It's who you know, not what you know.

"There's a lot of good, decent, hardworking people here. There's also a lot of conniving, deceitful, hypocritical people here and we probably have more churches per capita than, well, I don't know about Rome. It's the hypocrisy that gets me."

Charlie foresees great change and many problems coming with the influx of people now moving into the area from other places, primarily Florida.

"In my opinion, they've had their heads stuck in the sands here. There's no planning. It's the old school. Leave us alone. Don't mess with us. And that day is past whether you like it or not.

"I'm sure that some people here look at me as a smartass s.o.b. who's come up here to tell them how dumb they are. That's not so. We just report it straight. It's an experience, though. God, it's an experience."

The first white man to see the land on which Murphy one day

would be built was Hernando DeSoto, a Spaniard who came from Florida to explore the area in 1540. Nearly three centuries would pass before white men finally came to live among the Cherokees, whose land this was.

In 1830, Col. A.R.S. Hunter built an Indian trading post where the Valley and Hiwassee Rivers meet. That was the beginning of Murphy, then called Huntersville. Eight years later, Fort Butler was built at the settlement as headquarters for General Winfield Scott, who began rounding up the Cherokees to take them to the Indian territories of Oklahoma, a forced march that killed many and became known as the Trail of Tears.

The Cherokees' land was claimed by the state and parceled out to settlers in grants. Cherokee County was formed in 1839, and by the following year new settlers had pushed the population to nearly 3,500. Murphy, named for Archibald Murphy, a state political leader, was incorporated in 1851 as the county seat.

In 1865, the Cherokee County Courthouse was burned for the first time by Yankee raiders. It would burn four more times before the county built a courthouse of locally quarried blue marble blocks two-feet thick in 1927.

Murphy remained a country trading town for much of its existence. The construction of several TVA dams in the area brought prosperity in the '30s and early '40s, but only recent years have brought great change with the arrival of new industry, great numbers of tourists and new settlers from afar, many of them following the route DeSoto took.

Still, it is a small, remote country town with small country town ways. Young people cruise the downtown streets on weekend nights searching for excitement. The town has one aging theater, the Henn, and a new bowling alley and skating rink, but entertainment and social life revolve primarily around the churches and high school sports. Asheville, Chattanooga, and Atlanta are all 100 miles away.

A feeling of isolation has always been a part of life in Murphy. Georgia and Tennessee are nearby, and both their capitals are closer than Raleigh. "The only time we hear from Raleigh," people in Murphy like to say, "is during election year."

Dot Mason, who grew up in Asheville, well remembers what her father said when she told him she was thinking of marrying a young lawyer from Murphy and moving there with him. "Dot," he told her, "you're going to the end of the world."

"When I came here in 1951," she says, "there was only one industry. The only streets that were paved were U.S. 64 and U.S. 19-129. I have been here long enough to watch Murphy grow from an isolated community to a small country town and now to a small metropolis. What is frightening is we're growing too fast and we're not planning enough for it."

Some of that growth can surely be blamed on Dot, who as the

first full-time director of the Cherokee Chamber of Commerce has helped bring industry and people to Murphy and the county. In the 11 years since she joined the chamber, retail sales in the county nearly quintupled to more than $90 million annually.

At the new visitor center and chamber office on U.S. 64-19-129 that Dot got built completely with donations, more than 100,000 people signed the guest register and picked up material about the area last year. They came from every state and U.S. territory and 47 other countries. Many were looking for a new home. For those who are, Dot Mason is usually the first local person they meet.

"I tell them, 'Don't come to Murphy if you're a member of the jet set,'" she says. "This is no place for you. You're moving to a country town with country people. You make your own entertainment. It's church oriented."

Dot, whose husband is county attorney, doesn't believe tales of local political corruption. "It's a lot of talk. You know, sports is really big here. They're avid about sports. If you're from Murphy, you don't go to Andrews and lose your football game. They play football and all sports hard. Politics here is kind of like a football game. Republicans and Democrats play it just like football, but when it's over they go back to living with each other."

Dot has no regrets that she came to Murphy, "I raised my children here. They got good educations. They were qualified to go away to good colleges." Her son went to Wake Forest, her daughter to UNC-G. Both returned to Murphy to live. Her son is a district judge, her daughter a special education teacher.

"They didn't want to go anywhere else," says Dot. "They both love Murphy just as I do."

In 1974, when hippies were people to be feared in the mountains, a long-haired, bearded young man wandered into Murphy with a big pack on his back and half-Malamute dog named Cooper at his side. His name was Peter Jenkins and he had set out from New York to walk across America. In Robbinsville, in Graham County, he had been run out of town under threat of his life by local authorities, and he was now wary of the mountains and their people.

In Murphy, he was welcomed by the sheriff and taken in by a black family. He soon got a job in a sawmill and became close with a white mountain family.

He stayed four months, and after he left he wrote extensively about his experiences in Murphy in "National Geographic," "Reader's Digest," and in a 1979 best-selling book, "A Walk Across America."

The book portrayed the people of Murphy as warm and open.

"That's typical of the people," says Dot Mason. "They're just like that. They take in everybody, stray cats, dogs and people. Anybody who's traveling across the United States and stops in Murphy is going to get treated well."

213

The Final Miles

From Murphy, U.S. 64 still has 20 miles left on its journey through North Carolina. An easy 20 miles.

The highway is four lanes and the traffic is swift. The mountains through which it is cut are less than formidable, for the range begins petering out here.

People along this section of the highway depend a lot on tourists. Small motels, gas stations, restaurants, gift shops and sourwood honey stands are spaced along the way, not in gaudy excess, just available. The excess is in "See Rock City" and "Ruby Falls" signs. Ruby Falls signs give the mileage to that Chattanooga attraction every few miles.

Ranger sprawls over several miles, the last N.C. community on the highway shown on official state maps. It has a community center and a volunteer fire department, but it isn't the last community before the highway reaches Tennessee. That distinction goes to Hot House.

Not even the patriarch of Hot House knows how it came by its name. He is Hardie Tilson, known to neighbors as Hard. He is a hardy 93, and warm days are apt to find him sitting on the porch of his small house fast by the highway watching the traffic whiz by.

Hard was born and grew up about two miles from where he now lives. He lived 18 years in Murphy, following the carpentry trade, before he moved back to the community. He ran a small store, built a few houses, farmed a little.

"I lost my house when they built this four-lane highway," he says. "They took three acres and ever' building I had. I believe it was in '69. I had to get somebody to build this 'un. My wife was down, and I couldn't work much myself."

His wife, Florence, died in 1981.

"She stayed in a nursing home 10 year and she was down 12 year. I been by myself the last 14 year. I got no folks left a'tall. There was six of us boys and all of us is dead but me. One girl and she died when she was little. Me and my wife, we had one boy. He died in 1927, 13 years old. Doctor said it was Bright disease. I lived in Murphy when he took sick and died. I moved to Murphy to school 'im.

"The cemetery out here at Hopewell Church is full of my folks. That's where my wife and boy's buried, my daddy, my wife's mother, the man that partly raised me, my brothers, half brothers, all my friends. No tellin' how many's buried out there that I know,

214

Hard Tilson

helped bury. Uncles and aunts. That's where I'll be afore long, I reckon. Already got it fixed.

"Oh, it's a lonesome life to live by yourself. I'm too old to ever marry again. They's plenty of widder women all over the county, but I'm just too old. Like a ol' man when I lived at Murphy told me—he run a little store and I went up there a lot—his wife had died and he said there was another woman wanted to marry him. He said, 'But I couldn't love her, cause this ol' fool head wants a young woman.'"

Women from the church bring Hard's supper every day, and neighbors fetch him places he needs to go. He doesn't get out much, doesn't really care to. Things have changed so.

"It's like livin' in a new world to what it was when I was a boy. See, we was on ol' dirt roads, steer wagons, mule teams. It just ain't the same country. My half brother went to Kansas when he was a young man and raised his family there. He's dead now, but a few years ago he come back to visit and he didn't know where he was. That's how much the country's changed.

"Now all these Floridy people's a'comin' in here. They's none right around here, but they tell me there's a bunch of 'em back over that mountain there. It's a sight of traffic over there. Don't guess I'll have to worry about it, fer old age has got me till I ain't got the strength to do nothin' much.

"Just set here. I try to walk a little ever' day when the weather's favorable, but I'm afeared to get out there on that highway. It's fast, and at times it just a continual thing, and they don't seem to care about an old man."

Not far from Hard's house is the last restaurant before the highway leaves the state, appropriately a barbecue house. Herb's. Herbert Gibson and his wife, Helen, opened it in September 1982, just across and up the road from their brick house. Herb, who works in mine construction all over the country, had only cooked barbecue for parties before he decided to build the restaurant for his wife and son, Vaughn, to operate. He built the pit himself, from his own design, and there he and Vaughn cook hams, steer rumps and ribs the proper way, over hardwood coals, but the cut of the meat, the sauces and coleslaw served with it make it more akin to Tennessee-style barbecue than North Carolina.

From Herb's, the highway climbs over Franklin Gap, offering a view to the south and west as it descends. Climbing again, it passes Wolf Creek and the Carolina Motel, last motel before the Tennessee line, now owned by a Florida man.

Climbing still, the highway tops Angelico Gap, and ahead a raw vista opens: the barren, red, man-raped terrain that is the copper mining country of Tennessee, a nightmare of despoliation.

The state line follows the still lush ridge. On the Tennessee side is a package store, owned by former Florida residents, gaudy with colorful pennants and signs. This is where people from dry Cherokee County come to buy beer and fireworks.

Across the road, on the N.C. side of the highway, eastbound lane, the big "Welcome To North Carolina" sign stands in the front yard of the neat frame house where Hubert Jenkins lives with his wife, Willie, usually called Bill. Next to the house, close by the state line is their small cinder-block store. Their primary business is cigarettes, and on this day, a delivery day, they sit surrounded by cases and cases of cigarettes of almost every brand.

Because of tax differences, Hubert and Bill can sell cigarettes a dollar a carton cheaper than the place across the road. Tennessee smokers drive miles to buy cigarettes from them, but not the way they once did.

"Not like it used to be," Hubert says. "Cigarettes got so high. When I opened up cigarettes was $2.45 a carton. Look at 'em now. Seven dollars. They won't come from Chattanooga and buy cigarettes anymore. Used to, years ago, they'd come buy a case or something.

Not now. Business is just not like it was. You'd be surprised the people that have just quit smoking."

Still, business is good, and Hubert isn't complaining. He knew what he was doing when he bought this land 16 years ago. He knew it would give him a chance to get out of the mines where he worked for 33 years. He and Bill are right where they want to be, and they have no plans for leaving.

They don't consider themselves to be the last people in North Carolina, but the first.

"Reckon it just depends," says Hubert, "on which way you're going."

Index

East Woods Press Books

American Bed & Breakfast Cookbook, The
America's Grand Resort Hotels
Backcountry Cooking
Berkshire Trails for Walking & Ski Touring
Best Bed & Breakfast in the World, The
Blue Ridge Mountain Pleasures
California Bed & Breakfast Book, The
Campfire Chillers
Campfire Songs
Canoeing the Jersey Pine Barrens
Caribbean Bed & Breakfast Book, The
Carolina Curiosities
Carolina Seashells
Capentry: Some Tricks of the Trade from an
  Old-Style Carpenter
Catch-of-the-Day—Southern Seafood
  Secrets
Catfish Cookbook, The
Charlotte: A Touch of Gold
Coastal Ghosts
Complete Guide to Backpacking in Canada
Creative Gift Wrapping
Day Trips From Baltimore
Day Trips From Cincinnati
Day Trips From Houston
Day Trips From Phoenix-Tucson-Flagstaff
Drafting: Tips and Tricks on Drawing and
  Designing House Plans
Exploring Nova Scotia
Fifty Years on the Fifty: The Orange Bowl
  Story
From Whalebone to Hot House: North
  Carolina's Longest Highway, U.S. 64
Fructose Cookbook, The
Grand Old Ladies
Grand Strand: An Uncommon Guide to
  Myrtle Beach, The
Healthy Trail Food Book, The
Hiking from Inn to Inn: Maine to Virginia
Hiking Virginia's National Forests
Historic Country House Hotels in the U.K.
Home Exchanging
Hosteling USA, Third Edition
How to Afford Your Own Log Home
How to Play With Your Baby
Indiana: Off the Beaten Path
Interior Finish: More Tricks of the Trade
Jersey Shore, The

Just Folks: Visitin' with Carolina People
Kays Gary, Columnist
Maine Coast: A Nature Lover's Guide, The
Making Food Beautiful
Melancholy Bay, An Odyssey
Mid-Atlantic Bed & Breakfast Book, The
New England Bed & Breakfast Book, The
New England: Off the Beaten Path
North Carolina Is My Home
Ohio: Off the Beaten Path
Parent Power!
Parks of the Pacific Coast
Plain & Fancy Mustard Cookbook, The
Race, Rock and Religion
River Reflections
Rocky Mountain National Park Hiking
  Trails
Saturday Notebook, The
Sea Islands of the South
Separation and Divorce in North Carolina
South Carolina Hiking Trails
Southern Bed & Breakfast Book, The
Southern Rock: A Climber's Guide to the
  South
Sweets Without Guilt
Tar Heel Sights: Guide to North Carolina's
  Heritage
Tennessee Trails
Toys That Teach Your Child
Train Trips: Exploring America by Rail
Trout Fishing the Southern Appalachians
Vacationer's Guide to Orlando and Central
  Florida, A
Virginia: Off the Beaten Path
Walking From Inn to Inn: The San Francisco
  Bay Area
Walks in the Catskills
Walks in the Great Smokies
Walks with Nature in Rocky Mountain
  National Park
What To Do When You're Out Of It
What To Do With the Kids This Year
Whitewater Rafting in Eastern America
Wildflower Folklore
Wildflower Meadow Book, The
Woman's Journey, A
You Can't Live on Radishes

Order from:

The East Woods Press
429 East Boulevard
Charlotte, N.C. 28203
(704) 334-0897

For orders only, established accounts and charge card customers
may call our toll-free answering service:

(800) 438-1242, ext. 102   In N.C. (800) 532-0476